Oeasy to mak Organizers

Edited by Jeanne Stauffer

HOUSE of
WHITE
BIRCHES

PUBLISHERS
SINCE

Woodworking for Women™
Easy to Make Organizers

Copyright © 2005 House of White Birches, Berne, Indiana 46711
Woodworking for Women™ is a trademark of DRG Texas LP,
licensed for use by House of White Birches.

Editor: Jeanne Stauffer
Associate Editors: Sue Reeves, Dianne Schmidt
Technical Editors: Marla Freeman, Amy Phillips
Copy Supervisor: Michelle Beck
Copy Editor: Conor Allen

Photography Supervisor: Tammy Christian
Photography: Carl Clark, Christena Green, Matthew Owen, Nancy Sharp
Photography Stylist: Tammy Nussbaum

Art Director: Brad Snow
Publishing Services Manager: Brenda Gallmeyer
Graphic Arts Supervisor: Ronda Bechinski
Book Design/Graphic Artist: Amy S. Lin
Production Assistant: Cheryl Kempf, Marj Morgan
Traffic Coordinator: Sandra Beres
Technical Artists: John Buskirk, Pam Gregory

Chief Executive Officer: John Robinson
Publishing Director: David McKee
Marketing Director: Dan Fink
Sales Director: John Boggs
Editorial Director: Vivian Rothe
Publishing Services Director: Brenda R. Wendling

Printed in China
First Printing: 2005
Library of Congress Number: 2005900548
Hardcover ISBN: 1-59635-014-8
Softcover ISBN: 1-59635-037-7

Every effort has been made to ensure the accuracy and completeness of the instructions in this book. However, we cannot be responsible for human error or for the results when using materials other than those specified in the instructions, or for variations in individual work.

IMPORTANT SAFETY NOTICE: To prevent accidents, read instructions and use all safety guards on power equipment. Wear safety goggles and headphones to protect yourself. Do not wear loose clothing when working on power equipment. Due to the variability of construction materials and skill levels, neither the staff nor the publisher of Woodworking for Women books assume any responsibility for any accidents, injuries, damages or other losses incurred resulting from the material presented in this book.

Welcome

If there is one thing that most women want in today's world, it's a quiet, serene place where they can relax. Many of us are busy and on the go all day long. In the evening and on weekends, we are ready to cocoon, only to discover that our homes are cluttered and full of confusion.

In many cases, our homes are full of clutter because we simply don't have enough storage space. If that is the case for you, it's time for a change. It's time to take your hobby of woodworking and use it to make the great organizers in this book. We have super projects to help you organize every room of your home. From your entryway where you welcome friends and family, to your hobby room where you have several projects in process, we have just the right projects for you to make to unclutter your home and your life. Of course, the best part is that you get to spend time working with wood. What could be better than using your favorite hobby of woodworking to remove clutter from your home and simplify your life! Decide what room you want to start with and you're on your way to creating a simpler, more restful life. In addition to the 47 projects in the book, we sprinkled many helpful hints throughout on how to organize, so you can take life easy and enjoy it more.

Happy woodworking,

Jeanne Stauffer

CONTENTS

HOBBY AREAS

OFFICES

BED & BATH

ENTRIES

Welcome friends and family to your organized home with these useful projects for your entry. There's something for everyone, including the kids and dogs!

WELCOME HOME

Design by Anna Thompson

A beadboard back and two-tone finish give this hall tree, complete with under-seat storage, an upscale country look.

CUTTING

Note: Mark each piece as you begin the cutting process with chalk or a light pencil.

FRAMES

1 Rip two 1x6x72-inch poplar boards into two 2-inch-wide boards. With each board, make one pass, then turn the board over so the factory edge is against the table saw fence for the second pass. Mark two 2-inch lengths (A), one (D) and one (E). Mark one of the 1¼-inch "leftovers" (F). Set the other 1¼-inch remainder aside for now.

2 Rip the 1x4 poplar to 2-inch widths. Mark it (G) and set the remaining 1⅜-inch piece aside for now.

3 Rip another 1x6x72 to 2 inches and mark that piece (C), then widen the table saw cut to 2½ inches; put the factory edge against the fence and rip. Label this (B).

4 Cut the following with the miter saw: Back frame—cut the A boards to 70 inches for the back stiles, and the B and C boards to 36 inches for the rails; front frame—cut D to two rails 36 inches long and E to two stiles 17¾ inches long; side frames—cut F into four 17¾-inch stiles and G into four 14-inch rails.

LEG TAPER

1 On each of the 2-inch stiles, A and E, beginning at the bottom, measure in from the factory edge ¾ inch and make a mark. On the cut edge, measure up from the bottom 3 inches and mark the side. Draw a cutting line between these two points. Cut this angle on all four stiles.

PROJECT SIZE
43x70¾x18¼ inches

TOOLS
- Table saw
- Miter saw
- Jigsaw
- Router with ⅜-inch rabbeting, ⅜-inch roundover and ¼-inch cove bits
- Chisel
- Beadlock tenoning jig (optional: biscuit joiner or dowelling jig)
- Drill with ⅛- and ⅜-inch straight bits, and ⅜- and ½- inch Forstner or spade bits
- Square

SUPPLIES
- 1x4 poplar: one 6-foot length
- 1x6 poplar: five 6-foot lengths
- 1x8 cherry: two 8-foot lengths
- ⅜-inch beadboard: one 48x96-inch sheet
- Assortment of screws: ⅝-, 1¼- and 2½-inch
- ⅜-inch birch flush plugs
- Two 2½-inch butt hinges
- Wood glue
- ⅜-inch cherry flush plugs
- Six ½x5-inch birch shaker pegs
- Mirror: 36¾x14⅜ inches
- Glazier's points
- Sandpaper
- Deft oil finish
- Drill
- Silicone caulk
- Hunter green latex paint

2 On the 1¼-inch stiles (F), mark the bottom at ⅛ inch and the opposite side at 3 inches. Make the cuts.

FRAME ASSEMBLY

1 Lay out the frames as shown in the frame layouts diagram. For each of the frames, the rails will be butted into the sawn edge of the stile. This model was joined together using the Beadlock jig, which creates floating mortises and tenons. Join the stiles and rails of each frame in the

Organizing **TIPS**

Start with a plan. The reason many of us procrastinate when it comes to getting organized is that we know that it will get worse—in some cases, much worse!—before it gets better.

manner you have chosen, following manufacturer's instructions where available. Glue all joints, let dry, then sand smooth.

2 Rabbet the backs of each frame opening. These rabbets are ⅜ inch wide and ⅜ inch deep. Chisel out the corners.

3 Dry fit the mirror into the opening and make necessary adjustments.

4 Measure each of the panel openings from rabbet to rabbet, both vertically and horizontally. Reduce each measurement by ⅛ inch for easy fit. Measurements should be very close

to the following: middle back (H) 36⅝ x33⅜ inches; lower back (I) 36⅝x11⅞ inches; front panel (J) 36⅝x10⅞ inches; side panels (K) 14⅝x10⅞ inches. Cut panels from ⅜-inch beadboard.

5 Secure the middle back (H), both sides (K) and the front (J) with glue and ⅝-inch screws. Secure the bottom back (I) with screws only.

JOIN FRAMES

1 Butt the side frames into the front and back frames and attach with glue and predrilled, countersunk 2½-inch screws. Plug holes with ⅜-inch flush plugs. (Countersink with ⅜-inch Forstner bit driven ⅜ inch deep.)

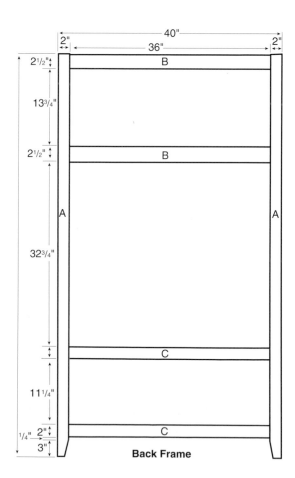

Back Frame

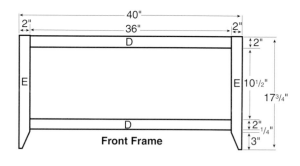

Front Frame

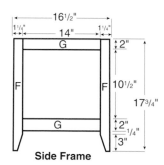

Side Frame

ASSEMBLY DIAGRAM

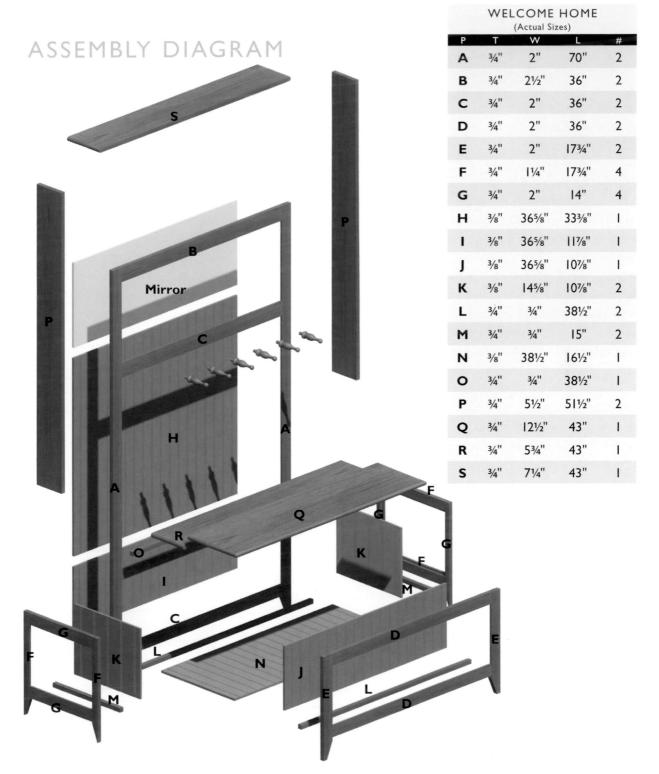

P	T	W	L	#
WELCOME HOME (Actual Sizes)				
A	¾"	2"	70"	2
B	¾"	2½"	36"	2
C	¾"	2"	36"	2
D	¾"	2"	36"	2
E	¾"	2"	17¾"	2
F	¾"	1¼"	17¾"	4
G	¾"	2"	14"	4
H	⅜"	36⅝"	33⅜"	1
I	⅜"	36⅝"	11⅞"	1
J	⅜"	36⅝"	10⅞"	1
K	⅜"	14⅝"	10⅞"	2
L	¾"	¾"	38½"	2
M	¾"	¾"	15"	2
N	⅜"	38½"	16½"	1
O	¾"	¾"	38½"	1
P	¾"	5½"	51½"	2
Q	¾"	12½"	43"	1
R	¾"	5¾"	43"	1
S	¾"	7¼"	43"	1

Note: *It is always a good practice to glue the plugs so the grain in the plug is running the same direction as the grain in the wood being plugged. Even though this unit will be painted, this is a great habit to get into for future projects.*

BOTTOM FRAMING

1 Rip the 1¼x72-inch and 1⅜x72-inch leftover poplar to ¾-inch widths.

2 Cut two cleats 38½ inches long (L) and two cleats 15 inches long (M).

3 Attach long cleats (L) to the bottom inside of the storage area, flush with the front and back frame bottoms. Then attach the short cleats (M) to the sides flush with the bottom. Predrill the holes and attach with 1¼-inch screws.

4 From ⅜-inch beadboard, cut the bottom (N) 38½x16½ inches. Fasten in place, resting on the cleats, with ⅝-inch screws.

5 From the leftover stock, cut a ¾x ¾-inch board to 38½ inches for the upper seat support (O). Fasten it to the sides with one 1¼-inch screw through the outside of each side into this upper seat support (flush with the top), beginning 5 inches in from the back of the unit. Predrill four ³⁄₁₆-inch holes into this seat support to attach the seat later.

6 Measure from the inside bottom of the mirror frame. Mark the following, then lightly square the lines down to the middle of the 2½-inch rail: 5³⁄₁₆, 10⁵⁄₁₆, 15⁷⁄₁₆, 20⁹⁄₁₆, 25¹¹⁄₁₆ and 30¹³⁄₁₆ inches. Cross these marks by measuring down 1¼ inches. With the ½-inch Forstner bit, drill a hole ⅜ inch deep at each of these six marks for the shaker pegs.

SEAT & TOP SHELF

1 From the 1x8 cherry, cut four pieces 43 inches long. Glue three together alternating the curve of the grain (check the ends). When dry, rip to 18¼-inch width (Q/R). The

remaining 1x8x43 is the top shelf (S).

2 Using the ⅜-inch roundover bit, bullnose (rout the top and bottom edges of) the sides, front, top and bottom of the seat (Q/R) and the top shelf (S).

3 With the back (flat) edge of the seat against the table saw fence, rip a 5¾-inch piece for the stationary seat back (R); the remaining 12½-inch piece will be piece Q. Hinge these two pieces back together, mortising the hinges into the seat edges.

UPRIGHT SUPPORTS
Note: *If the thickness of the cherry is not ¾ inch, adjust the length of side upright (P) accordingly.*

1 Cut the remaining 1x6x72-inch boards to 51½ inches for the upright supports (P). Beginning 6½ inches up from the bottom and ending 3 inches from the top, rout a decorative ¼-inch cove into both sides of the front edge of each support.

2 Beginning ⅝ inch in from the outside edge of the back and with the tops flush, attach the upright supports by predrilling and countersinking 1⅝-inch screws in from the back. Countersink only so the head of the screw is flush with the back.

FINISH & FINAL ASSEMBLY

1 Using clear, natural Deft oil, oil cherry seat and top shelf, tops of the cherry plugs, and birch shaker pegs. Let cure.

2 Paint hall tree *hunter green*. Avoid getting paint into the holes drilled for the shaker pegs.

3 Glue shaker pegs in place on back rail.

4 Install seat (Q) by predrilling and countersinking 1¼-inch screws up into the seat through the cleats, flush with the back of the unit and evenly spaced on the sides. Also secure seat to upper seat support (O) in the same manner—flush with the front of the back seat board.

5 Install top shelf (S) by predrilling and countersinking into the back and uprights. Plug holes with cherry plugs.

6 Install mirror into top cutout. Secure with several glazier's points along each rabbet, then seal with a bead of silicone caulk over the points and against the wood frame. ✦

Organizing **TIPS**

No room for a workshop? Convert a seldom-used closet into a mini-workshop by lining walls with Peg-Board for lightweight tools. Build sturdy shelves for heavier tools and add some drawers underneath. Attach a sturdy folding work surface to the inside of the door. Build it with good strong legs that fold out when you lower it.

READY TO GO

Design by Loretta Mateik

A bone-shaped peg rack hanging by the back door keeps dog-walking essentials close at hand.

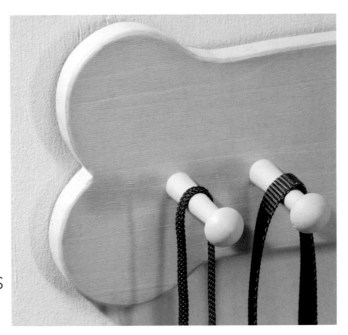

PROJECT NOTES

This functional project can even be personalized with your pet's name.

INSTRUCTIONS

1 Trace bone pattern onto folded paper; unfold and copy full-size pattern onto 1x8 using graphite paper. Include placement of peg holes.

2 Cut along lines with the jigsaw or scroll saw.

3 Using router and roundover bit, round front edge of bone cut out.

4 Drill holes for pegs. *Note: The hole placement may be adjusted to your needs. The spacing for the pegs on this rack was designed to hold a toy as well as the leashes.*

5 Sand rough edges and wipe clean.

6 Basecoat bone-shaped base and the shaker pegs with two thin coats of *antique white*, letting dry after each coat. *Note: This process may raise the grain of the wood. If so, lightly sand surfaces and wipe clean between coats.*

7 Very lightly shade around the top edge of the bone with *sable brown*.

8 Glue shaker pegs in holes. Let dry.

9 Finish with several light coats of matte spray sealer.

10 Attach hanging hardware. ◆

PROJECT SIZE
13½x6¼x3¾ inches

TOOLS
- Jigsaw or scroll saw
- Drill with ½-inch Forstner bit
- Router with ⅛-inch roundover bit

SUPPLIES
- 1x8 white pine: 2 feet
- Tracing paper
- Graphite paper
- Sandpaper
- Four 3⅝-inch Shaker pegs
- DecoArt Americana acrylic paint: antique white #DA58 and sable brown #DA61
- Paintbrushes
- E-6000 glue (wood glue)
- DecoArt Americana matte spray sealer
- Hanging hardware

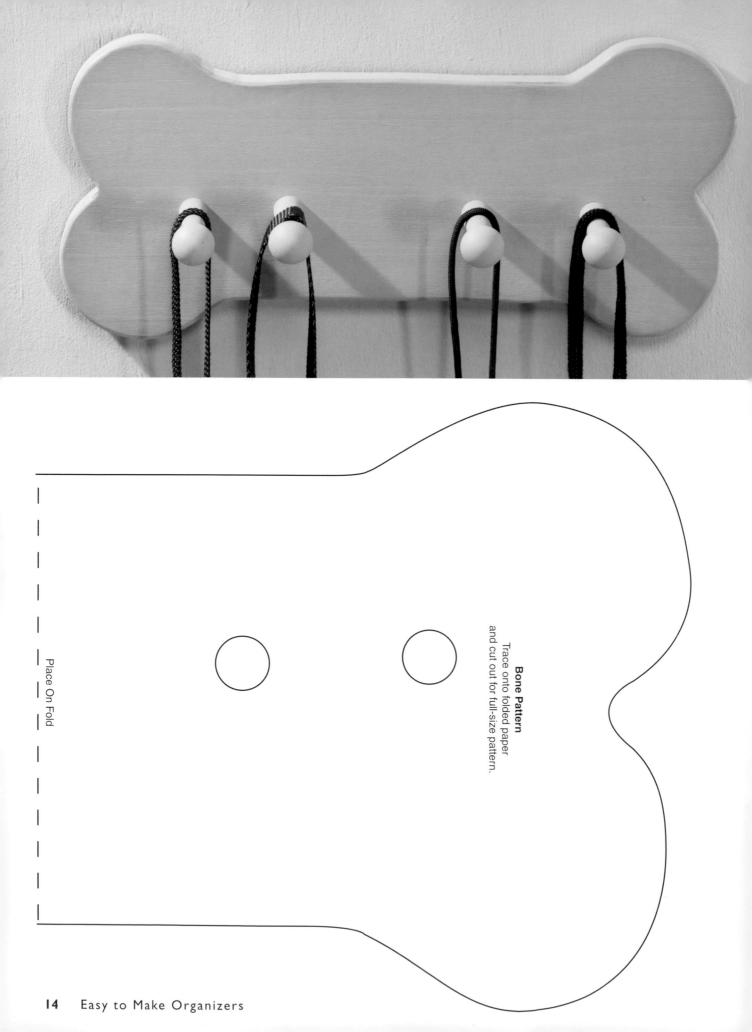

Place On Fold

Bone Pattern
Trace onto folded paper
and cut out for full-size pattern.

KID'S CLUTTER KEEPER

Design by Loretta Mateik

Keep track of shoes, library books and backpacks with this colorful three-piece set.

Book box

CUTTING

1 Cut the ½-inch plywood to a 15-inch length for back, two 7-inch lengths for sides, one 11-inch length for the front and one 10-inch length for the bottom.

2 Rip the 15-inch back to 11 inches wide.

3 Rip the 11-inch front and both 7-inch sides to 8 inches.

4 Rip the 10-inch bottom to 7 inches.

5 Glue and nail the box together with the sides butting into the back and front, then slide the bottom in place.

6 Round over the front edges of the back piece, the top outside edges of the box and the two front corners with router and ⅛-inch roundover bit.

7 Miter both ends of a piece of the Colonial trim to 11 inches, long point to long point, for front piece.

8 Cut two pieces, mitered on only one end so they mirror each other, to 7½ inches long point to long point for side pieces.

9 Basecoat all pieces with equal parts *deep burgundy* and *crimson tide*. Sand, wipe clean and repeat.

10 Add trim to top of front and sides with glue and brad nails.

Book box

PROJECT SIZE
11x15x8 inches

TOOLS
- Table saw
- Brad nailer with ¾-inch nails
- Router with ⅛-inch roundover bit
- Miter saw

SUPPLIES
- ½-inch birch plywood: 1x5 feet
- ⁷⁄₁₆x⁷⁄₁₆ embossed beaded Colonial trim: one 3-foot length
- DecoArt Americana acrylic paints: deep burgundy #DA128, crimson tide #DA21 and titanium white #DA01
- Paintbrushes
- Sandpaper
- Wood glue
- Wood filler
- Tracing paper
- Transfer paper
- Stylus
- DecoArt Americana matte spray finish/sealer #DAS13

11 Fill all nail holes. Let dry, sand and wipe clean. Touch up with basecoat.

12 Using the stylus, transfer number/letter patterns onto front with tracing and transfer paper. Apply lettering with *titanium white*.

13 Seal with several coats of matte spray finish/sealer.

Shoe box

CUTTING

1 Cut the ½-inch plywood to a 16-inch length for front, two 17-inch lengths for top and bottom, and two 8¾-inch lengths for the sides.

2 Rip the 16-inch front and both 8¾-inch sides to 8 inches.

3 Rip both 17-inch top and bottom pieces to 8 inches.

4 Basecoat all pieces with equal parts *deep burgundy* and *crimson tide*. Sand, wipe clean and repeat.

5 Assemble box with glue and brad nails. Sides butt into top and bottom. Insert front and nail in place.

6 Fill all nail holes. Let dry, sand and wipe clean. Touch up with basecoat.

7 Using the stylus, transfer number/letter patterns onto top with tracing and transfer paper. Apply lettering with *titanium white*.

8 Seal with several coats of matte spray finish/sealer.

Message board

CUTTING

1 If purchased pieces of the ⅛-inch plywood and the dry-erase board are larger than the sizes listed, cut them to size now. Set the table saw fence to 17 inches and cut both plywood and dry-erase board to width.

2 Move the fence to 15 inches and cut the ⅛-inch backer.

3 Move the fence again to 9½ inches and cut the dry-erase board to length.

Shoe box

PROJECT SIZE
17x9¾x8 inches

TOOLS
- Table saw
- Brad nailer with ¾-inch nails

SUPPLIES
- ½-inch birch plywood: 1x8 feet
- DecoArt Americana acrylic paints: deep burgundy #DA128, crimson tide #DA21 and titanium white #DA01
- Paintbrushes
- Sandpaper
- Brad nails
- Wood glue
- Wood filler
- Tracing paper
- Transfer paper
- Stylus
- DecoArt Americana matte spray finish/sealer #DAS13

Message board

PROJECT SIZE
17x15x3 inches, including pegs

TOOLS
- Table saw
- Router with ⅛-inch roundover bit
- Drill with ½-inch Forstner bit
- Miter saw
- Clamps
- Brad nailer with ¾- and ½-inch brads

SUPPLIES
- ⅛-inch plywood*: 15x17 inches
- 1x6 pine: 2 feet
- ⁵⁄₁₆x1³⁄₁₆-inch checkerboard trim molding: 4 feet
- ¼x1¹¹⁄₁₆-inch rope trim molding: 3 feet
- Dry-erase board: 9½x17 inches**
- ½-inch wood dowel: 1 foot
- Two 1¼-inch wood balls
- Wood glue
- Wood filler
- DecoArt Americana acrylic paints: deep burgundy #DA128 and crimson tide #DA21
- Paintbrushes
- Sandpaper
- DecoArt Americana matte spray finish/sealer #DAS13
- Hardware to hang

*This is sometimes called "bending" plywood.
**You may have to purchase a larger piece of dry-erase board, perhaps even a full 4x8 foot sheet.

Organizing TIPS

Attach a towel rack to the footboard of your child's bed. She can hang tomorrow's clothes there, ready to jump into in the morning.

4 Cut the 1x6 to 17 inches.

5 With the ⅛-inch roundover bit, rout the top perimeter of the 1x6.

6 On the 1x6, measure down from each side 3¼ inches and in from each side 4¼ inches. "X" where these measurements cross. Drill a ½-inch hole, ⅜ inch deep at each mark.

7 Drill a ½-inch hole ⅝ inch deep into each wood ball.

8 Cut two dowel pieces to 2-inch lengths. Glue dowel pieces into wood balls.

Checkerboard trim

Option 1: Lay out the checkerboard

Organizing **TIPS**

Do tiny game parts mysteriously disappear from their box? Glue a small resealable plastic freezer bag to the inside of the box to provide safe and secure storage.

trim on top of the dry-erase board. Look at the corners and center the trim so that the top trim and the side trim will match. Mark the top at the corners and cut the 45-degree angle to match those marks. Now cut the angle on each side piece so it matches the design at the corner of the top piece.

Option 2: Cut the side trim first so there remains 1 inch of the raised block at the top long point. Measure from corner to corner between the side trim pieces. Cut the miter on one end of the top piece so that, at the long point, 1¼ inches of the raised block is intact. Cut the other corner as the first with the angle opposite, and cut the block just past the length of the measurement. Shorten the top, if necessary, by cutting out material in the middle and making the top piece two mirrored pieces.

Rope trim

1 Cut the top piece to 17 inches (long point to long point) with both ends mitered.

2 Cut the sides to length 5⅝ inches (long point) with the top mitered and the bottom square.

PRE-ASSEMBLY

1 Glue and clamp the dry-erase board to the backer board flush at the top and sides.

FINISH

1 Basecoat all pieces except dry-erase board with equal parts *deep burgundy* and *crimson tide*. Sand, wipe clean and repeat.

ASSEMBLY

1 Glue and clamp the 1x6x17 onto the ⅛-inch backer board, butted up against the dry-erase board.

2 Lay out the checkerboard trim, confirm the fit, then glue and nail in place with ½-inch brad nails. (Should they happen to come through to the back, just trim off with wire snips.)

3 Lay out the rope molding on the 1x6. The top trim should extend beyond the top of the 1x6 to keep the dry-erase marker from rolling off the ledge. Glue and nail in place.

4 Fill all nail holes. When dry, sand then lightly touch up with basecoat.

5 Glue wood balls and dowels in place.

6 Mask off dry-erase board and spray on sealer/matte finish. Coat several times.

7 Attach appropriate hardware for hanging.

8 Place dry-erase marker pen on shelf created by the 1x6. ✦

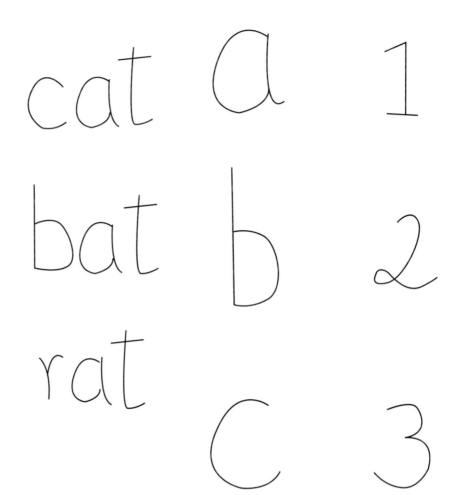

Shoe Box Lettering

Book Box Lettering

HANGING CATCH-ALL

Design by Anna Thompson

Kids can stow backpacks, mittens and hats in these cubbies, instead of tossing them on the floor.

CUTTING

1 From the 8-foot 1x8, use miter saw to cut one 36¼-inch length for top (D), one 32¾-inch length for peg rail (C) and two 7¾-inch lengths for dividers (E).

2 From the 6-foot 1x8, use miter saw to cut two 13-inch lengths for sides (B) and one 33⅜-inch length for shelf (A).

3 Using table saw, rip the width of each piece as follows: top (D) to 7¼ inches wide; sides (B) to 6½ inches wide; shelf (A) and dividers (E) to 6¼ inches wide; and peg rail (C) to 5 inches wide.

4 Determine which edge of each side (B) will be to the front. Transfer curve template onto the bottom front end of each side; cut with jigsaw.

5 Referring to Fig. 1, use router with ¾-inch straight bit to rout a dado ⅜ inch deep for the shelf on the inside of each side, beginning 7⅝ inches from the top.

6 Maintaining the ⅜ inch depth, set the router guide so ¼ inch of material will be cut away. With the router base sitting on the width (not thickness) of the board, rout rabbets in the bottom back of the top board (D) beginning and ending 1⅜ inches from each end (Fig. 2), and on the inside back of each side piece (B) beginning at the top and ending 8⅛-inches down (Fig. 1).

7 With the depth still at ⅜ inch, set the guide to cut out ½ inch and rabbet the bottom back of the shelf (A) the entire length.

8 Change the router bit to the ⅜-inch roundover bit and rout the top and bottom of the sides and front of the unit top to create a bull-nose effect.

PROJECT SIZE
36¼x13¾x7¼ inches

TOOLS
- Miter saw
- Table saw
- Jigsaw or scroll saw
- Router with ⅜-inch roundover bit and ¾-inch rabbeting (or straight) bit
- Square
- Drill with ⅜- and ½-inch Forstner bits, ¹⁄₁₆- and ⅛-inch bits, and #4 countersink

SUPPLIES
- 1x8 maple: one 6-foot length and one 8-foot length
- ¼-inch maple plywood: 2x4 feet
- Graphite paper
- Sandpaper
- Wood glue and brushes
- Five maple shaker pegs
- Twenty 1⅝-inch drywall screws
- Twenty ⅜-inch maple plugs
- Eight to twelve ¾-inch flat head screws
- Deft clear wood finish
- Hanging hardware

9 Sand all cut edges thoroughly.

ASSEMBLE

1 Dry-fit shelf (A) into dadoes cut into the sides (B). The back of the shelf should be even with the inside edge of the rabbets, and the front edges of the shelf and sides should be flush. Set the peg rail (C) in place under the shelf and into the shelf rabbet. If the peg rail is too long, cut it to fit. Disassemble.

2 Find the center of the peg rail. Using a square, draw a light pencil line across the width of peg rail (C). Measure from this center line each direction 5⁷/₁₆ inches and 10¾ inches. Using square, draw light lines on rail for peg placement. Measure up from the bottom of the rail 2¼ inches at each line and make a cross mark. With the ½-inch Forstner bit, drill ⅝-inch-deep holes at each cross (+).

3 Glue in the shaker pegs.

4 Brush glue lightly into the side dadoes and insert the shelf. Predrill and countersink two 1⅝-inch drywall screws through the sides and into the ends of the shelf.

Note: *The countersinking in steps 5–7 is done with the ⅜-inch Forstner bit drilled ⅜ inch deep. This makes a hole perfectly suited for the maple plugs.*

5 Brush glue into the shelf dado and insert peg rail into that dado and butted into the sides. The back of the peg rail and the back of the

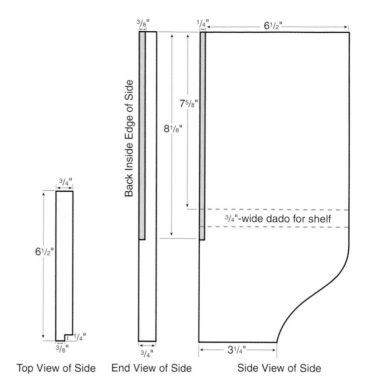

Fig. 1
Rout a ¾"-wide dado for shelf on inside of each side.
Rout a ⅜"-deep by ¼"-wide rabbet on inside back of each side.

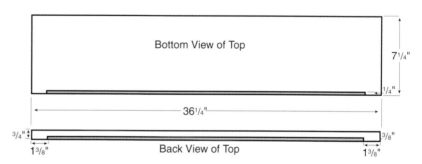

Fig. 2
Cut a ¼"-wide dado ⅜" deep on bottom back edge of top (D).

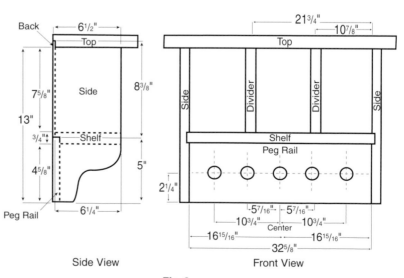

Fig. 3

ASSEMBLY DIAGRAM

HANGING CATCH-ALL
(Actual Sizes)

P	T	W	L	#
A	¾"	6¼"	33⅜"	1
B	¾"	6½"	13"	2
C	¾"	5"	32¾"	1
D	¾"	7¼"	36¼"	1
E	¾"	6¼"	7¾"	2
F	¼"	8¾"	33⅜"	1

sides should be flush. Predrill and countersink two 1⅝-inch drywall screws through the sides and into the ends of the peg rail.

6 Center the top (D) so the back of the top and the back of the sides are flush, and the overlap at each end is the same. (This should be just over 1 inch.) Predrill and countersink two 1⅝-inch drywall screws through the top and into each side.

7 Measuring on the inside, mark the bottom of the top at 10⅞

Organizing **TIPS**

Clutter can't be contained! Spend 15 minutes every day decluttering, and you'll be amazed at how organized you can become!

inches and 21¾ inches. Repeat these measurements (from the same side) marking the top of the shelf. Center the dividers (E) vertically at each of these sets of marks (Fig. 3). Predrill and countersink 1⅝-inch screws into each of the dividers—two up through the shelf and two down from the top.

8 Glue maple plugs in each countersunk hole. Be careful to place them so the grain is running the same way as the grain being plugged.

9 Measure the dimensions of the back rabbets side-to-side and top-to-bottom. Cut the ¼-inch maple ¹⁄₁₆

inch less in height and width for back (F); install into the back of the unit. Secure with glue and ¾-inch flat-head screws. Predrill and countersink the screw holes with the ¹⁄₁₆-inch bit and #4 countersink bit.

FINISH

1 Sand unit thoroughly, making sure the plugs are sanded flush. Finish with at least three coats of Deft clear wood finish following manufacturer's instructions.

2 Attach appropriate mounting hardware of your choice. ✦

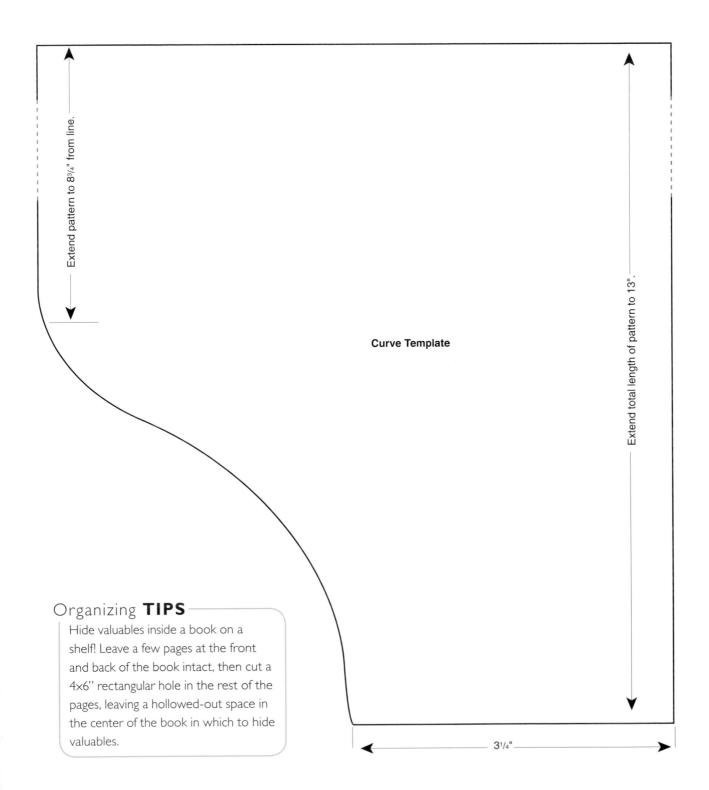

Extend pattern to 8³/₄" from line.

Curve Template

Extend total length of pattern to 13".

3¹/₄"

Organizing **TIPS**

Hide valuables inside a book on a shelf! Leave a few pages at the front and back of the book intact, then cut a 4×6" rectangular hole in the rest of the pages, leaving a hollowed-out space in the center of the book in which to hide valuables.

YESTERDAY'S
TULIPS

Design by Delores Ruzicka

Think spring! Lightly distressed tulips bloom atop this simple shelf unit.

PROJECT NOTES

When driving a screw into pine without predrilling, make sure that the heads of the screws are driven flush with the unit surface. This will cover better when painting. You may also wish to use a small amount of spackle or wood filler to fill the screw heads prior to painting.

PROJECT SIZE

22½x39x11¼ inches

TOOLS

- Circular or table saw
- Jigsaw
- Sander

SUPPLIES

- 1x12 pine: one 8-foot length; one 10-foot length
- Tracing paper
- Graphite paper
- Sandpaper
- Wood glue
- 1½-inch drywall screws
- Vinyl spackle or wood filler
- Acrylic paint: white, red, light green, dark green and pale yellow
- Paintbrushes
- Light oak stain

CUTTING

1 Using circular saw, cut 1x12 into two 24-inch lengths (sides), three 21-inch lengths (top, bottom and shelf) and two 39-inch lengths (back).

2 Trace tulip pattern onto tracing paper, joining left and right sides and extending lines at bottom of pattern 3½ inches. Use graphite paper to transfer tulip pattern to top of one back piece for right back. Flip pattern over to reverse it and transfer to remaining back piece for left back. Cut out tulip designs with jigsaw.

3 Sand edges smooth; remove dust.

ASSEMBLE & FINISH

1 Use glue and 1½-inch drywall screws to attach sides to ends of bottom piece with edges flush; attach shelf between sides 12 inches from bottom. This should center your shelf in the unit. If it does not, make the appropriate adjustments.

2 Attach top to ends of sides flush at the top, using glue and 1½ inch drywall screws. Fill screw heads with spackle or wood filler. Let dry. Sand flush.

3 Using photo as a guide, paint as follows, applying multiple coats as needed to cover and letting dry after each coat:
Shelf base—Paint with *white*.
Tulips—Paint with *red* and *pale yellow*; add dots and comma strokes for detail.
Leaves—Paint with *light green*; shade and outline with *dark green*. Add random dots with *dark green*.

4 Lay unit down on its face. With bottom and outer edges flush, attach back pieces to back of shelf base (top, sides and bottom) using glue and drywall screws.

5 Lightly sand edges of tulip design and shelf base. Apply light oak stain to sanded edges. Use a stiff-bristled brush to spatter light oak stain randomly onto shelf base. ◆

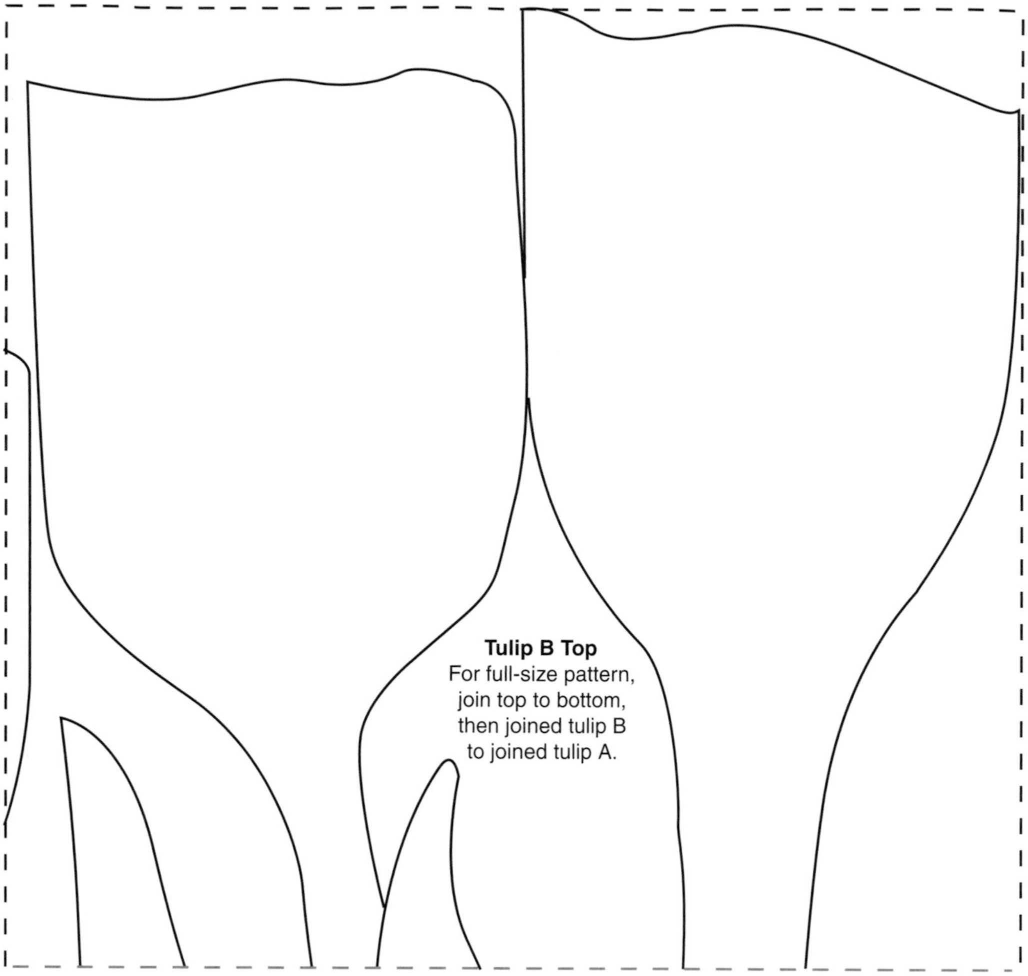

Tulip B Top
For full-size pattern,
join top to bottom,
then joined tulip B
to joined tulip A.

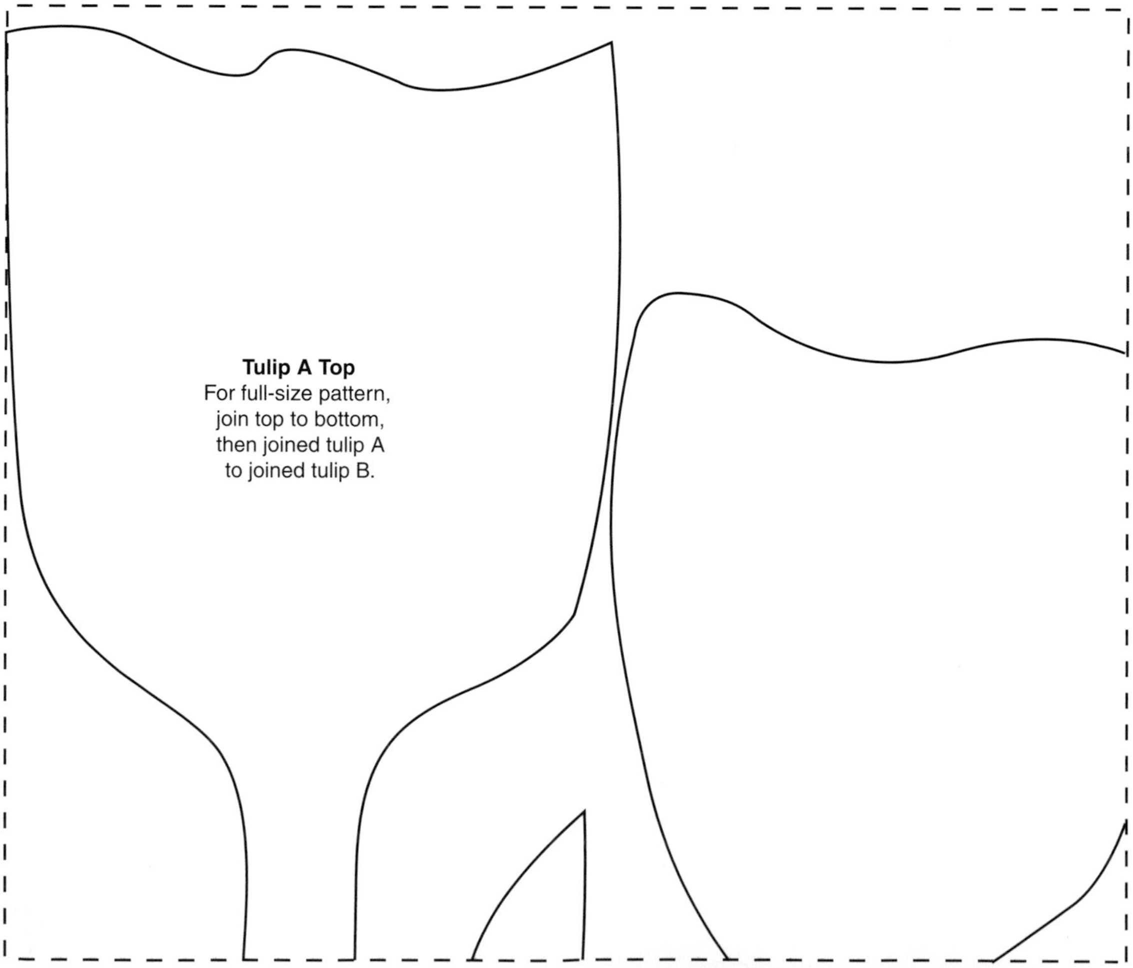

Tulip A Top
For full-size pattern,
join top to bottom,
then joined tulip A
to joined tulip B.

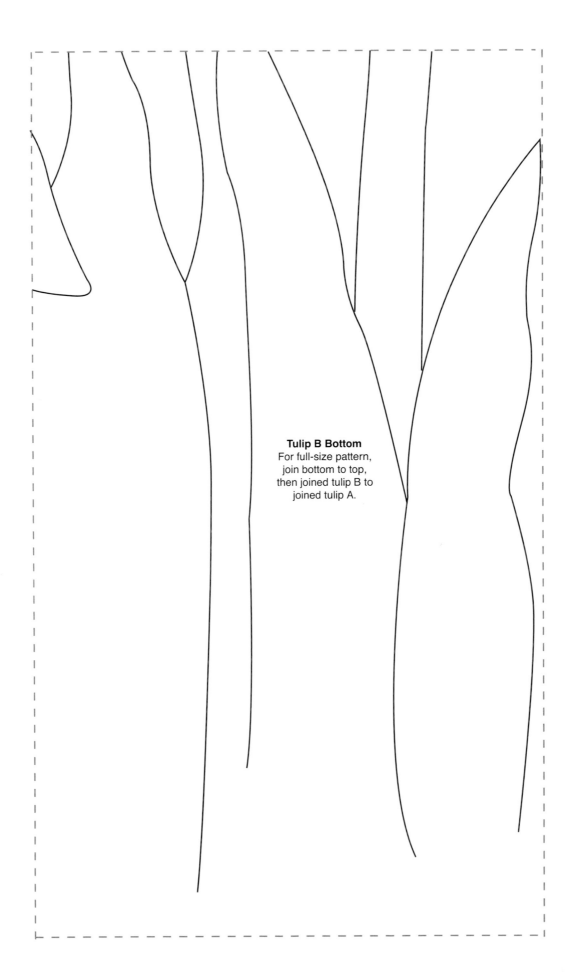

Tulip B Bottom
For full-size pattern,
join bottom to top,
then joined tulip B to
joined tulip A.

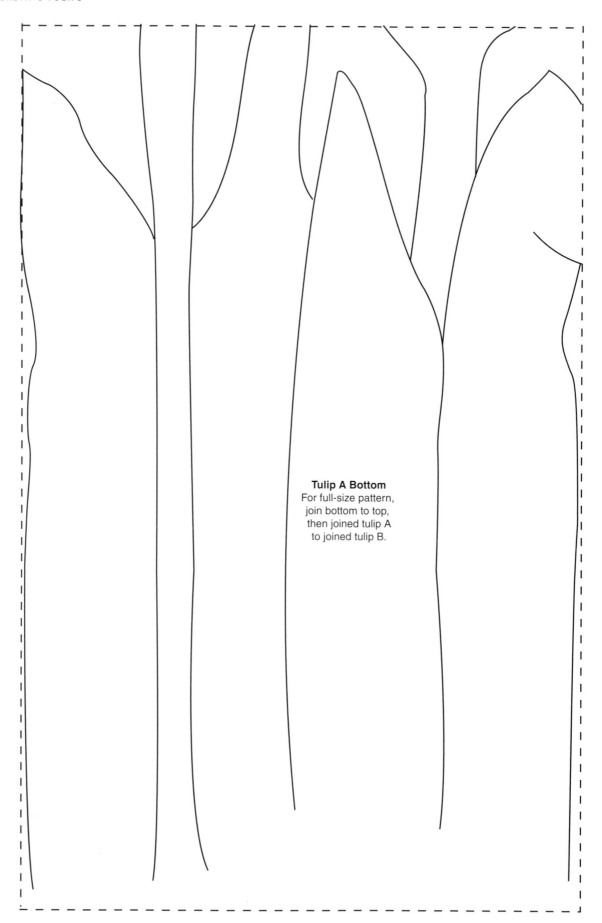

Tulip A Bottom
For full-size pattern,
join bottom to top,
then joined tulip A
to joined tulip B.

HANG YOUR HAT

Design by Bev Shenefield

Unique cabinet pulls add flair and personality to a small, quick-to-finish project.

INSTRUCTIONS

1 Measure 1½ inches from corners on each side of redwood. Draw a line across corners connecting marks; cut off corners on lines (Fig. 1).

2 With router and ¼-inch roundover bit, round all front edges.

3 Referring to Fig. 2, drill four ¹¹⁄₆₄-inch holes in redwood. Use straight edge to mark each Woodsies from corner to corner (Fig. 3); drill an ¹¹⁄₆₄-inch hole in each Woodsies where lines intersect.

4 Use sander and 150-grit paper to sand all surfaces of redwood until smooth. Hand-sand Woodsies with 150-grit sandpaper. Remove dust.

5 Glue Woodsies to front of redwood, aligning holes. Remove any excess glue; let dry.

6 Use 1-inch brush to apply clear satin finish to all surfaces; let dry two hours. Hand sand with 220-grit sandpaper; remove dust. Repeat process, then apply a third coat of finish. Let dry.

7 Attach ring hangers to upper edge of back with wood screws, placing each hanger 3 inches from each end.

8 Place washer over machine screw and insert screw through back of redwood, tapping gently with hammer through redwood, but using screwdriver to turn screws through Woodsies.

9 Place cabinet pull over screw on front; tighten with screwdriver, being sure all pulls are in upright position. ✦

Organizing **TIPS**

Save the cardboard rolls from toilet paper and paper towels and tuck folded scarves into them. Line them up neatly in a drawer.

PROJECT SIZE
18x5½x1½ inches, excluding hooks

TOOLS
- Power saw
- Router with ¼-inch roundover bit
- Drill with ¹¹⁄₆₄-inch bit
- Palm sander with 150-grit paper
- Metal straight edge
- Phillips screwdriver

SUPPLIES
- 2x6 smooth common redwood: 18 inches
- Four Forster Woodsies XXL (¹⁄₁₆x2x2-inch) wooden squares

- Sandpaper: 150- to 220-grit
- Crafter's Pick Sand 'N Stain wood glue
- Minwax polycrylic clear satin finish
- 1-inch soft brush
- Two professional ring hangers
- Four #6x¾ Phillips wood screws
- Four ⅛x¾-inch fender washers
- Four 8-32x2-inch round-head slotted machine screws
- Four twig-shaped cabinet pulls*

Model project was made using cabinet pulls #P17030V-PBL-C from Home Depot.

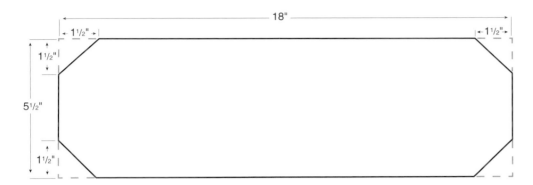

Fig. 1
Cut corners diagonally.

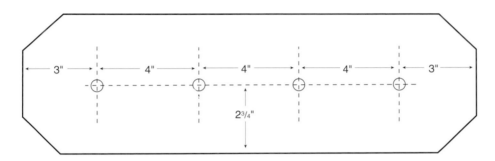

Fig. 2
Mark placement of holes.

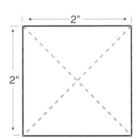

Fig. 3
Mark center of
each Woodsie.

Organizing **TIPS**

Paint or decorate an old bike basket, then hang it on the outside wall next to your front door. When you get home with your arms full, you can put your packages in the basket until you've found your keys and unlocked the door.

FAMILY ROOMS

You'll be able to relax and enjoy your neat and tidy living spaces after you've built some of these useful organizers. From CD and book storage to larger units for electronics and bulky items, there's something for every home.

POGO'S TOY CHEST

Design by Loretta Mateik

Teach your pal to pick up toys and drop them into this box. You'll have a neater living area, and he'll love learning a new trick!

PROJECT NOTE

To check any unit for squareness, measure from corner to corner diagonally, first one set of corners, then the other set. If the unit is square, both measurements will be the same.

PROJECT SIZE
15½x14¾x15½ inches

TOOLS
- Table saw
- Miter saw
- Jigsaw or scroll saw
- Brad nailer
- Drill

SUPPLIES
- ¼-inch Baltic birch plywood*: 36x48 inches (grain running with the 48-inch side)
- ¾-inch stainable wood stock*: twelve 15-inch lengths (option: 1x8x36 inches ripped to 1-inch widths)
- ⅛-inch Baltic birch plywood: 8x11 inches
- ¾-inch pine outside corner molding: 12 feet
- ½-inch Baltic birch plywood: 16x16 inches
- ¾-inch pine screen molding: 5 feet
- Graphite paper
- Wood glue
- ⅝-inch brads
- Sandpaper
- DecoArt Americana water-based stain: maple #AMS11
- 1¹⁄₁₆x30-inch Stanley continuous hinge (piano hinge)
- Wood filler
- DecoArt matte sealer/finisher spray
- 7½-inch Stanley lid support

*Measurements given are actual, not nominal. Standard nominal lumber will need to be ripped and/or planed to size.

CUTTING

1 From ¼-inch birch, use table saw to cut two 14x14½-inch pieces (A) for base sides, two 14x15-inch pieces (B) for base front and back, and one 14½x14½-inch piece (C) for base bottom. *Note: Cut so grain runs with the 14-inch side for all four A and B pieces.*

2 Rip ¾-inch stock to 1-inch widths on the table saw. With the miter saw, cut four 14½-inch pieces (D) for frame front and back, four 13-inch pieces (E) for frame sides, and four 12-inch pieces (F) for frame corner supports.

3 Using graphite paper, transfer patterns for lettering, dog and ball onto the ⅛-inch birch plywood. Cut with a jigsaw or scroll saw.

4 From outside corner molding, use miter saw to cut the following pieces: four 15½-inch pieces with a 45-degree miter at each end (G) for lid trim, and four 13⅞-inch pieces with straight cuts at each end (H) for base vertical trim. *Note: If lid measures greater than 15x15 inches, adjust lengths of (G) pieces accordingly, adding ½-inch to lid*

measurements for an accurate long-point measurement.

ASSEMBLE & FINISH

1 Butt base sides (A) into base front and back (B); glue and nail together with the brad nailer and ⅝-inch brads (Fig 1). Glue and nail the base bottom (C) into place with the brad nailer and ⅝-inch brads. ***Note:*** *If the bottom piece is square, it will bring the sides into square.*

2 Referring to Fig. 2, dry-fit frame pieces inside base as follows: (D) along the front and back at the top and bottom, (E) at the sides top and bottom, and (F) between the bottom frame and the top frame at the corners. All four top pieces should be flush with the top edge of the sides and front. Make adjustments as necessary. Glue and nail frame in place, nailing from the outside with the ⅝-inch brads.

3 For lid (I), place the ½x16x16-inch birch plywood squarely on the top of the base and mark its outline from underneath with a pencil. Cut along pencil lines. ***Note:*** *Lid should very nearly measure 15x15 inches.*

4 Sand base and lid; wipe clean. Stain project, inside and out, with DecoArt maple water based stain according to manufacturer's instructions. Let dry.

5 Cut a 13-inch piece of the Stanley continuous hinge. Predrill holes and attach hinge to lid and back as shown in Fig. 3, using the screws

included with the hinge. ***Note:*** *Attach the hinge on the ends first, then predrill the remaining holes.*

6 Trial-fit lid trim pieces (G) to outline the lid and base vertical trim pieces (H) to base corners. Make necessary adjustments, then glue and nail in place. ***Note:*** *The back lid trim piece covers the hinge; be sure to keep that edge free from glue, and only nail from the top into the back piece.*

7 Measure the distance between the edges of the outside corner molding horizontally along the bottom of the box. Cut four pieces (J) of screen molding to these lengths (about 14 inches). Lightly sand the edges of the screen molding (J) to soften, then use glue and ⅝-inch brads to attach to bottom edge of box flush with the bottoms of the base vertical trim pieces (G). There will be about a ⅛-inch space between the bottom of the molding and the bottom of the box.

8 Fill all nail holes on trim pieces only. Let dry. Sand excess filler from nail holes and smooth any rough edges on embellishments.

9 Glue cutout embellishments to base as desired, using photo as a guide. Let dry.

10 Apply several light coats of DecoArt matte sealer/finisher spray as instructed by manufacturer.

11 Attach lid support hardware according to manufacturer's instructions. ✦

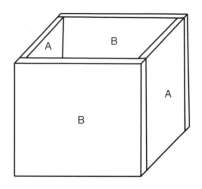

Fig. 1
Butt base sides (A) into base front and back (B).

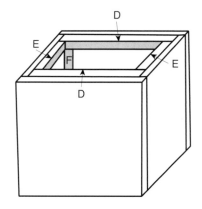

Fig. 2
Attach frame pieces inside of base.

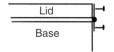

Fig. 3
Attach hinge to lid and back of base.

POGO'S TOY CHEST
(Actual Sizes)

P	T	W	L	#
A	¼"	14"	14½"	2
B	¼"	14"	15"	2
C	¼"	14½"	14½"	1
D	¾"	1"	14½"	4
E	¾"	1"	13"	4
F	¾"	1"	12"	4
G	¾"	¾"	15½"	4
H	¾"	¾"	13⅞"	4
I	½"	15"	15"	1
J	¾"	¾"	14"	4

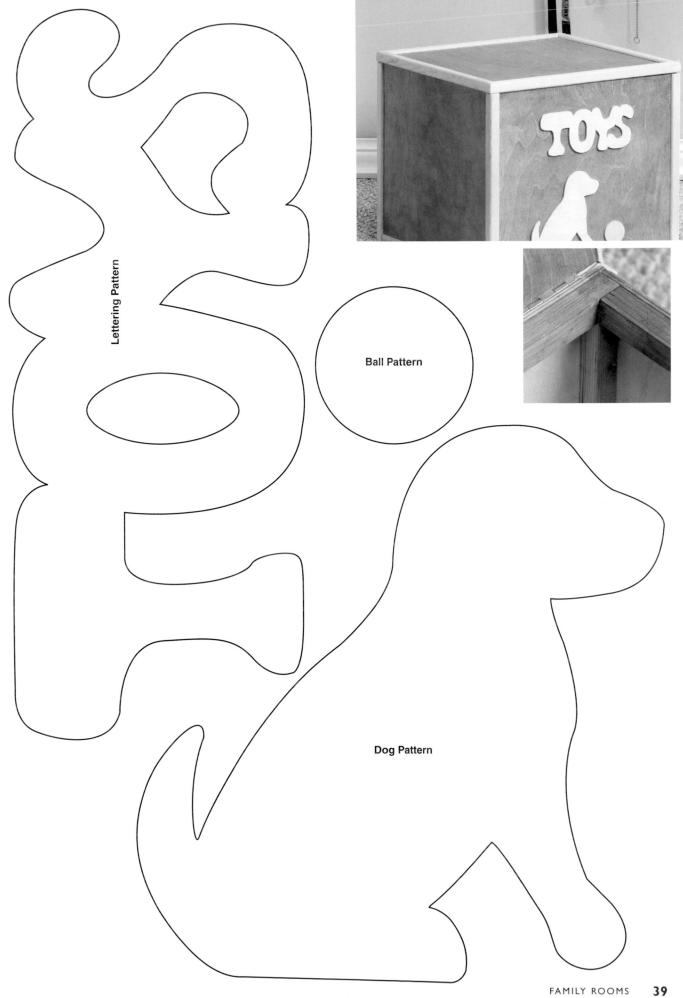

Lettering Pattern

Ball Pattern

Dog Pattern

THE BASKET BARN

Design by Anna Thompson

Fill this cabinet with baskets to store blankets, clothes, games, hobby supplies, toys … the stuff of life!

FRAME MILLING

1 From two of the 8-foot 1x4s, use miter saw to cut four 46-inch lengths. On the table saw, rip each of these to 2 inches wide for front/back stiles (B). **Note:** *Set the four leftover widths aside.*

2 On table saw still set for 2-inch wide cut, rip the 1x6 two times, turning the board over so the factory edge is against the fence for the second pass. **Note:** *Set the leftover width aside.*

3 Place all the 2-inch-wide pieces together with the factory edge down; sand off the saw marks.

4 Measure the four leftover widths that were set aside in step 1. If needed, rip to 1¼-inch widths for end stiles (D).

5 Cut the ¾x2x120-inch boards into four 36-inch lengths for front/back rails (A) and four 13-inch lengths for end rails (C).

6 From ¾-inch birch plywood, cut one 17x40-inch piece for the top (I), one 15½x38½-inch piece for the bottom (L), two 14½x38½-inch pieces for shelves (P) and one 16x7¼-inch piece for jig base (Jig A). Cut a 1-inch square notch out of the two back corners of each shelf (P).

7 From the leftover 1¼-inch width from step 2, cut two 36½-inch lengths for shelf trim (O).

8 Rip the remaining 8-foot 1x4 into ¾-inch-wide strips. Cut the ¾-inch-wide strips into four 38½-inch lengths for front/back cleats (G) and four 14-inch lengths for end cleats (H), one 8-inch length for shim (Jig D), and four 14½-inch lengths for horizontal supports (N).

9 From 4-foot 1x2, cut two 16-inch lengths for jig clamps (Jig B) and one 7¼-inch length for router guide (Jig. C).

PROJECT SIZE
41½x46¾x17¾ inches

TOOLS
- Miter saw
- Table saw
- Jigsaw
- Sander
- Doweling jig
- Router with ⅜-inch rabbeting bit
- ½-inch chisel
- Drill with ⁵⁄₁₆-inch bit and #4 countersink bit, and ⅜-inch countersink bit (or Forstner bit)

SUPPLIES
- 1x4 poplar: three 8-foot lengths and one 4-foot length
- 1x6 poplar: one 10-foot length
- ¾-inch birch plywood: 4x8-feet
- 1x2 poplar (for jig): 4 feet
- ⅜-inch beadboard: 4x8-feet
- ⁵⁄₁₆-inch wooden dowels
- Wood glue
- ⅝-inch screws
- 1¼-inch screws
- ⅜-inch maple flush plugs
- Rustoleum colonial red paint
- Paint brushes

LEG TAPERS

1 Taper the bottoms of the front/back stiles (B) by marking the inside edge of each stile 4 inches from the bottom; mark the bottom ¾ inch from the outside edge. Draw a line between these points and cut with table saw or jigsaw (Fig. 1).

2 Taper the end stiles (D) in the same manner, but marking bottom edge only ⅛ inch from outside edge (Fig. 1).

3 Sand cut edges.

CASE FRAMES

1 Referring to Fig. 2 and assembly diagram, layout case frames by assembling the front/back rails (A) with the front/back stiles (B), and the end rails (C) with the end stiles (D). **Note:** *Be sure the taper at the bottom of each stile is toward the inside.*

2 Dowel the frames together with glue and two ⁵⁄₁₆-inch wooden dowels in each joint (Fig. 2).

3 On the inside of the back frame and both side frames, rout a rabbet ⅜ inch wide and ⅜ inch deep using the ⅜-inch rabbeting bit. **Note:** *The front frame does not need to be rabbeted.* Chisel the corners square.

PANELS

Note: *Measurements given are for model project. For precise fit, measure routed frames and cut panels to fit.*

1 From ⅜-inch beadboard, cut two 13¾x38¾-inch pieces for ends (F) and one 36¾x38¾-inch piece for back (E). **Note:** *Cut so the bead runs with the 38¾-inch side.*

2 Dry-fit the panels in the frames, with the bead of the beadboard facing in on the back panel and out on the end panels. Make any necessary adjustments, then glue and fasten with ⅝-inch screws, predrilled and countersunk.

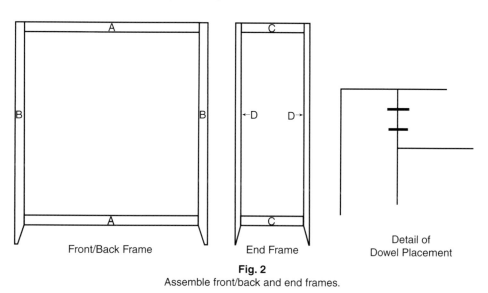

Fig. 2
Assemble front/back and end frames.

Front/Back Frame   End Frame   Detail of Dowel Placement

Fig. 1
Cut tapers on inside edges of stiles.

Front/Back Stile (B)   46" (extended)   End Stile (D)
2"   1¼"
4"   4"
¾"   ⅛"

Fig. 3
Frame case inside at top and bottom with cleats flush with rails and stiles.

Top/Bottom View
¾"   38½"   ¾"
¾"   1¼"
17"
2"   40"   2"

ASSEMBLY DIAGRAM

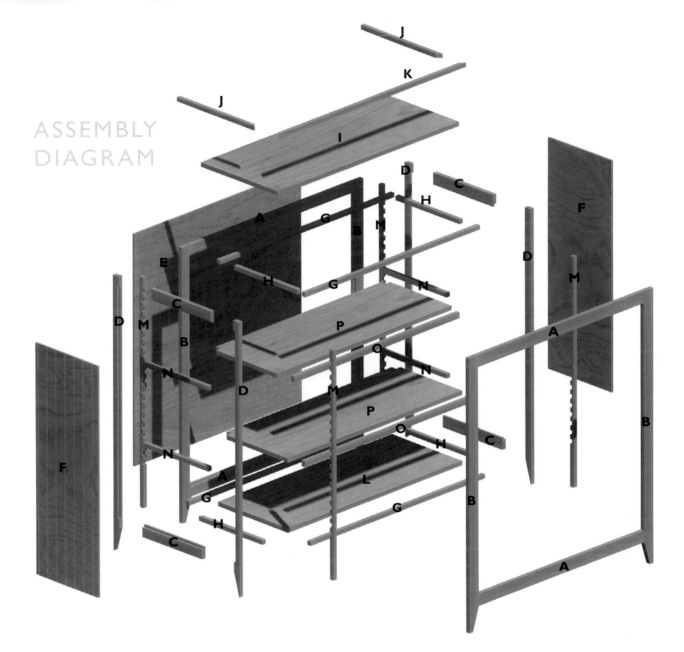

THE BASKET BARN				
(Actual Sizes)				
P	T	W	L	#
A	¾"	2"	36"	4
B	¾"	2"	46"	4
C	¾"	2"	13"	4
D	¾"	1¼"	46"	4

E	⅜"	36¾"	38¾"	1
F	⅜"	13¾"	38¾"	2
G	¾"	¾"	38½"	4
H	¾"	¾"	14"	4
I	¾"	17"	40"	1
J	¾"	¾"	17¾"	2

K	¾"	¾"	41½"	1
L	¾"	15½"	38½"	1
M	¾"	¾"	38½"	4
N	¾"	¾"	14½"	4
O	¾"	1¼"	36½"	2
P	¾"	14½"	38½"	2

CASE ASSEMBLY

1 Glue frames together by butting the sides into the front and back, then secure by predrilling and countersinking 1¼-inch screws.

2 Plug the holes with ⅜-inch flat plugs.

3 Use front/back cleats (G) and end cleats (H) to frame the inside of the box flush with top and bottom rails. Predrill holes and attach cleats to frame with glue and 1¼-inch screws (Fig. 3).

TOP & BOTTOM

1 Cut remaining ¾x¾-inch strips to fit around sides and front of top

(I) as follows: two 17¾-inch lengths for top side trim (J), each mitered on one end, and one 41½-inch length for top front trim (K), mitered at both ends. Attach trim to top with glue and 1¼-inch screws (countersunk). Plug holes with ⅜-inch plugs.

2 Center top on unit side-to-side with back edges flush. Drive 1¼-inch screws through the cleats into the bottom of the top to attach.

3 Place unit on its back. Referring to assembly diagram, set the bottom (L) in place and secure by driving 1¼-inch screws through the cleat and into the bottom board from underneath the unit.

SHELVES

1 Referring to Fig. 4, use 1¼-inch screws to attach one jig clamp (Jig B) to bottom long edge of jig base (Jig A).

2 Set in in the remaining 4-foot 1x4 poplar board and fasten remaining jig clamp (Jig B) on opposite long edge of jig base to hold the 1x4 in place. Screw the router guide (Jig C) to jig clamps across 1x4 (M).

3 Beginning 2 inches from end of 1x4, use router with a ¾-inch straight bit

set to cut ⅜ inch deep to rout first dado across 1x4, working in direction of arrow (Fig. 4) and cutting dado through both 1x2 jig clamps (Jig B).

4 Remove 1x4 from jig. Place ¾x ¾x8-inch shim (Jig D) across jig clamps and against router guide. Using same bit and setting on router, make a reference cut by routing through first 1x2 jig clamp. Remove shim.

5 Replace 1x4 in jig. Line up first dado with reference cut just made on jig; cut a second dado. Move 1x4 up, aligning second dado with reference cut, and make a subsequent cut. Repeat down the length of the 1x4 to within 6 inches from the end.

6 Remove dadoed 1x4 from jig and cut length to 38½ inches. Rip into four ¾-inch-wide strips for vertical supports (M).

7 Install vertical supports (N) in inside corners using glue and predrilled 1¼-inch screws. Insert horizontal shelf supports (N) into vertical supports.

8 Attach shelf trim (O) to front edges of the shelves (P) with glue and countersunk 1¼-inch screws, beginning and ending 1 inch from the end of the shelf (Fig. 5).

9 Trial-fit the shelves onto shelf supports; adjust fit as necessary.

FINISH

1 Sand surfaces and edges smooth, making sure all plugs are sanded flush. Remove dust.

2 Paint with *colonial red*, following manufacturer's instructions. ◆

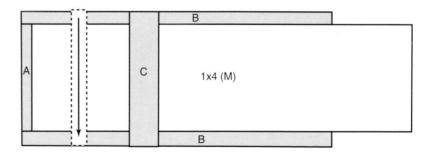

Fig. 4
Use jig to cut vertical supports (M).

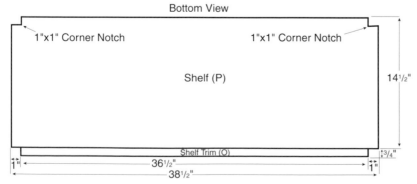

Bottom View

Fig. 5
Attach shelf trim (O) to shelf (P).

JIG CUTTING CHART
(Actual Sizes)

P	T	W	L	#
A	¾"	16"	7¼"	1
B	¾"	1½"	16"	2
C	¾"	1½"	7¼"	1
D	¾"	¾"	8"	1

HANDY CD STACKER

Design by Joyce Atwood

Keep that pile of CDs or DVDs organized and within easy reach. Let a child join you in the shop for a fun and productive afternoon of woodworking.

PROJECT SIZE
19½x11½x7¼ inches

TOOLS
- Table saw or circular saw
- Awl or nail
- Drill with ⅜-inch bit
- Router with ¼-inch roundover bit (optional)
- Clamps

SUPPLIES
- 1x8 pine: 24 inches
- ⅜-inch wooden dowel: six 18½-inch lengths
- Sandpaper: medium- and fine-grit
- Wood glue
- DecoArt Americana Water-Based Stain Conditioner #DSA33
- DecoArt Americana mahogany #AMS09 water-based stain
- DecoArt DuraClear satin varnish #DS21
- Paintbrush
- Soft cloth

INSTRUCTIONS

1 From 1x8, cut two 11½-inch lengths for ends.

2 Place dowel placement template on one end piece and mark placement of dowels using an awl or nail for right-hand end piece. Flip template over and place on second end piece and mark in same manner for left-hand end piece.

3 Drill a ⅜-inch hole ⅜ inch deep at each mark.

4 If desired, use router with ¼-inch roundover bit to round edges of end pieces. If router is not available, a sander may be used.

5 Sand all pieces smooth; remove dust. Glue ends of dowels in holes. Clamp together until dry.

6 Lightly dampen the surface with water and let dry. Sand surface with medium- then fine-grit sandpaper and remove dust. Apply stain conditioner with a brush; let set five minutes, then remove excess with a soft cloth. Let dry 30 minutes. Sand lightly and remove dust.

7 Apply three coats of mahogany stain with a soft cloth, letting dry 3 hours between coats. When completely dry, apply satin varnish following manufacturer's directions. ✦

Align this edge with top edge of end piece for top rack.

+

Dowel Placement Pattern
Transfer placement of dowels
for top rack, then reposition
pattern and transfer placement
of dowels for bottom rack.
Flip pattern to transfer marks
to opposite end.

+

+

Align this edge with bottom edge of end piece for bottom rack.

Organizing **TIPS**

Use a canvas over-the-door shoe organizer to keep kids' toys corralled in
the car. Cut in half and hemmed, the
organizer can be tied to the back of the
driver's seat to keep toys within reach.

ADJUSTABLE BOOK BENCH

Design by Anna Thompson

Organize books and use up leftovers at the same time! It's a win-win situation.

CUTTING

1 Rip 1x8 oak to 6-inch width, then cut to three 8-inch lengths.

2 Cut 1½x1½ inches off the front corners at a 45-degree angle.

3 Rout both sides of the front, back and top of all three pieces with chamfer bit (or cut 45-degree bevel on table saw).

4 Draw a line across one board, ⅝ inch up from the bottom from front to back. Measuring from the front, mark this line at 1, 3, 5 and 7 inches. Drill all the way through this piece at each of these four marks. This is the center board.

5 Using this piece as a template, draw the drill locations on the other two boards. With the ⅝-inch bit, drill these holes ⅝ inch deep. Be careful not to drill through these two pieces.

6 Cut oak dowels into four 16-inch lengths.

ASSEMBLE & FINISH

1 Place glue in holes of one end and insert dowels. Slide center over dowels, then glue remaining end in place.

2 Clamp until dry.

3 Finish with three coats of spray lacquer, sanding between coats. ✦

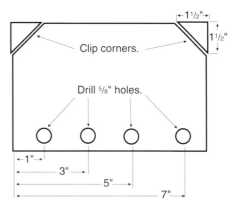

**Corner Cuts &
Hole Placement**

PROJECT SIZE
16½x6x8 inches

TOOLS
- Table saw
- Miter saw
- Router with chamfer bit
- Drill with ⅝-inch bit
- Two 24-inch-long clamps

SUPPLIES
- 1x8 oak: one 3-foot length
- ⅝-inch oak dowels: two 3-foot lengths
- Wood glue
- Sandpaper
- Spray lacquer

COMMAND PERFORMANCE

Design by Anna Thompson

Router detailing on the door and contrasting square plugs add sophistication to simple CD storage.

PROJECT SIZE
10x32⅝x10 inches

TOOLS
- Planer
- Table saw
- Router with ½-inch straight, ⅜-inch cove and ⅜-inch roundover bits
- Drill with ⅜-inch Forstner bit and ⅛-inch straight bit
- Clamps

SUPPLIES
- 1x8 oak: one 6-foot and one 8-foot length
- 1x10 oak: one 4-foot length.
- 1- and 2-inch screws
- ⅜-inch oak flush plugs
- Wood glue
- 1½-inch nonmortise hinges: 3
- Sandpaper
- Deft clear wood finish

CUTTING

1 Plane the 1x8 oak to ½-inch thickness and the 1x10 to ⅝-inch thickness.

2 Cut the ⅝-inch oak into two 9¼-inch lengths and two 8¼-inch lengths. Rip the 8¼-inch boards to 8¼-inch squares.

3 Rout a ⅜-inch cove around the perimeter of the 8¼-inch boards and round over the top and bottom edges of the 9¼-inch boards.

4 Cut the ½-inch thick oak to the following: three pieces to 29¾ inches for use in step 5, one piece to 29½ inches for door and three pieces 6⅞ inches for use in step 5.

5 Rip all three of the 6⅞-inch pieces to 6¼ inches for shelves along with two of the 29¾-inch pieces for the sides. If needed, rip the final 29¾-inch piece to 7¼ inches for the back.

6 From the remaining ⅝-inch stock, cut four pieces 2⅛ inches square for feet. With the ⅜-inch roundover bit, round two sides of each foot.

CUTTING THE SHELF DADOES

Cut three dadoes in each side for the shelves ¼ inch deep and ½ inch wide. The tops of the dadoes will be at 6, 12½, and 20½ inches measured from the top of the sides.

FLUTING THE DOOR

1 Flute the door with the ½-inch straight router bit. Centered 1½ inches in from each side and beginning and ending 4½ inches from the top or bottom, rout the two outside flutes on the door panel.

2 Beginning and ending 3 inches from the top or bottom, rout the middle flute right down the center of the door.

ASSEMBLE & FINISH

1 Attach the sides to the back (sides butt into back) with glue and countersunk 1-inch screws. Predrill with ⅛-inch bit and countersink with the ⅜-inch Forstner bit and plug the holes with the ⅜-inch oak flush plugs.

2 Apply glue to dadoes and slide shelves in place. Clamp in place until the glue dries. Clean up all glue runs immediately.

3 For the top, center and glue a 9¼-inch-square board over an 8¼-inch-square board, making sure the cove edge of the 8¼-inch-square

board is at the bottom.

4 For the base, center and glue the other 8¼-inch-square piece over the other 9¼-inch-square piece, making sure the cove side of the 8¼-inch-square piece is at the top.

5 Center the top on the top of the pedestal and lightly draw a line outlining the sides and back. Turn the top upside down and predrill through to the top inside the outline. Turn the top right side up and predrill through the top and into the sides and back. Countersink the holes, then attach with the 2-inch screws. Repeat for the

base at the bottom of the pedestal. Glue the oak flush plugs in place, making sure the grains run the same direction. (For a contrast option, square plugs could be used.)

6 Glue the four feet to the bottom corners of the base so there is a ½-inch reveal (see photo above).

7 Install three 1½-inch nonmortise hinges to hang the door, centering it from top to bottom.

8 Sand thoroughly and finish with three coats of Deft clear wood finish. ✦

LEISURELY
AFTERNOON

Design by Angie Kopacek

Oak plywood helps speed the construction on this easy-to-customize case, so you can spend more time using it.

CUTTING

1 Cut the two 4x8-foot ¾-inch oak plywood sheets according to cutting diagram. Label each piece with chalk, as well as inside/outside, left/right, front/back.

2 From 24x24-inch sheet, cut divider (A) 18 inches wide (cross grain) by 20 inches high (with grain).

JOINERY PREP

1 Band the following with the iron-on banding: the front edge of the top (D) and bottom (C), the front edges of the sides (E)—the top and bottom will be banded after the dadoes are cut, the front edge of the divider (A), the front edge of the stationary shelf (B) and all four edges of the adjustable shelves (H and I).

2 Mark the locations of each biscuit. Slots will be located at the side edges of the top, bottom, stationary shelf and divider. Matching slots will go into the inside of the sides, the bottom of the stationary shelf and the top of the bottom. The top will be flush to the top of the sides and the bottom flush to the bottom of the sides. (See biscuit diagram.)

3 Set the biscuit joiner to cut a slot centered on the thickness of the plywood. Cut the slots for the biscuits. See biscuit diagram. Be sure the slots of adjoining pieces line up properly.

SHELF SUPPORT DADOES

1 On the inside of one side, measure in from the front 6 inches. Cut a dado ½ inch wide by ¼ inch deep from the top to ⅛ inch up from the biscuit row for the stationary shelf. For the lower section, measure in 2½ inches from the front, and cut a dado of the same size from ⅛ inch below the biscuit row of the stationary shelf to bottom of the side.

PROJECT SIZE
36x60x18 inches

TOOLS
- Circular saw
- Iron
- Biscuit joiner
- Plunge router with ½-inch straight bit
- Fixed base router with ⅜-inch rabbet bit
- Chisel
- Carpenter's square
- Drill with ¼-inch bit

SUPPLIES
- ¾-inch oak plywood: two 4x8-foot sheets
- ¾x24x24-inch oak plywood
- ½x48x96-inch oak plywood
- ¾-inch iron-on oak edge banding: 77 feet
- Biscuits
- Shelf standard strips and supports
- Four inset hinges WSC #124231
- Two knobs WSC #130162
- Magnetic door catches (optional)
- Chalk
- Wood glue
- Small nails or ½-inch screws
- Stain or dye
- Water-based polyurethane

2 On the same side board, measure in 2½ inches from the back and cut the same dado from top to bottom.

3 Repeat steps 1 and 2 on the other side board.

4 Iron on oak edge banding to the top and bottom of each side.

5 On the vertical divider, measure in 2½ inches from the front and 2½ inches from the back and cut dadoes from the top to the bottom. Do this to both sides of the divider.

CASE ASSEMBLY

1 Dry-fit the case together. The horizontal shelf and the vertical divider should be flush with the front of the sides and bottom, and ½ inch short in the back. Check for squareness by measuring diagonally from corner to corner. If the measurement is the same, the unit is square. Make any necessary adjustments, then glue the case together.

2 Using the rabbetting bit, rout a rabbet ⅜ inch wide and ½ inch deep around the inside perimeter of the back of the unit. Chisel out corners.

3 Measure rabbet area and cut ½-inch plywood for back (F) to fit. Glue in place and let dry. Back should be close to 35¼x59¼ inches.

SHELF SUPPORTS

1 Install shelf standards referring to Shelf Support Diagram. Be sure the standards line up for level shelves. Find a common reference point, like measuring up from the bottom or down from the top and cut the

lengths accordingly. Even use a square and square across from the front edge at a set measurement, but see that the holes in the shelf standard are in the same place for the sides and the vertical standard. Attach with small nails or ½-inch screws—especially in the vertical divider where your standards are back to back and only separated by ¼ inch of plywood.

DOORS

1 Measure the opening between the bottom and the stationary shelf, and from the vertical divider to the side. Subtract ⅛ inch from each measurement and cut the ¾-inch plywood for the doors (G). This should be close to 16¾x20.

2 Band the outside edge of each door and install hinges.

ASSEMBLY DIAGRAM

LEISURELY AFTERNOON
(Actual Sizes)

P	T	W	L	#
A	¾"	17½"	20"	1
B	¾"	17½"	34½"	1
C	¾"	18"	34½"	1
D	¾"	18"	34½"	1
E	¾"	18"	60"	2
F	½"	35¼"	59¼"	1
G	¾"	16¾"	20"	2
H	¾"	15"	34¼"	2
I	¾"	16½"	16⅞"	2

3 Install each door to inside of cabinet side, centering vertically.

4 Band the remaining edges.

5 Drill a ¼-inch hole through each door for the knob. Place the hole 3 inches down from the top and 3 inches in from the side opposite the hinges. ***Note:*** *The size of the drill bit may vary based on the screw diameter of the doorknobs chosen.*

FINISH

1 Stain the case following the manufacturer's instructions. Model project was dyed with Transfast powder dye on light oak.

2 Topcoat with a water-based polyurethane. Apply at least two coats—three is recommended.

3 Attach knobs. Attach magnetic door catches if you like. ✦

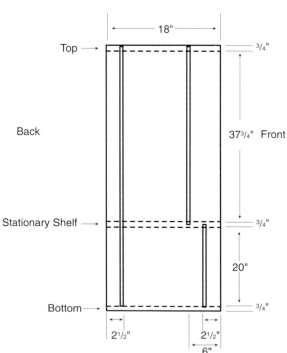

Shelf Support

Centered
³/₈" from top

Inside

Back

60"

Centered
21¼" from bottom

Centered
³/₈" from bottom

18"

Biscuit Placement on Sides

17¼"

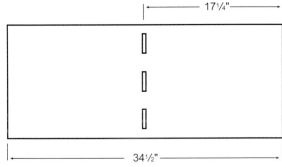

34½"

**Bottom of Stationary Shelf
and Top of Bottom Shelf**

**End View of Divider, Stationary
Shelf, Bottom and Top**

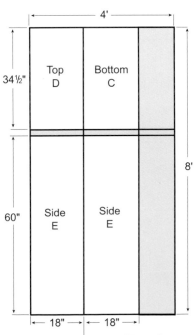

4'

34½"

Top
D

Bottom
C

8'

60"

Side
E

Side
E

18"   18"

Cutting Diagram Sheet One

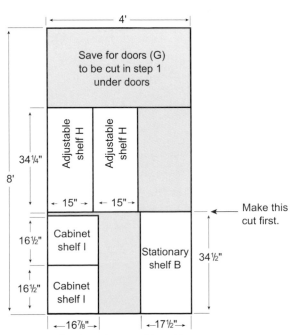

4'

Save for doors (G)
to be cut in step 1
under doors

34¼"

Adjustable
shelf H

Adjustable
shelf H

8'

15"   15"

16½"

Cabinet
shelf I

Make this
cut first.

34½"

16½"

Cabinet
shelf I

Stationary
shelf B

16⅞"   17½"

Cutting Diagram Sheet Two

AMONG MY SOUVENIRS

Design by Cindy Reusser

Display your treasured memories from family vacations in these easy-to-make cubbies.

PROJECT SIZE
12x9x7¼ inches each

TOOLS
- Table saw or miter saw
- Nail set

SUPPLIES FOR SET OF FOUR
- 1x8 pine: one 6-foot length and one 8-foot length
- Sandpaper
- Wood glue
- 1½-inch finish nails
- Pre-stain wood conditioner
- Oil-based interior stain
- Wood filler to match stain
- Hardware for hanging

Organizing **TIPS**

Use inexpensive paper plates between pieces of china to cushion them and prevent scratching.

PROJECT NOTE
Supplies and instructions given are for four cubby holes.

INSTRUCTIONS

1 From 1x8, cut eight 7½-inch lengths (A pieces) and eight 12-inch lengths (B pieces).

2 Sand all pieces.

3 Place two A pieces upright on flat work surface for sides. Glue and nail one B piece to top edges of sides for cubbyhole top. Flip piece over and glue and nail a second B piece to opposite edges of sides for cubbyhole bottom.

4 Repeat step 3 for remaining A and B pieces to make a total of four cubbyholes.

5 Sand assembled units; remove dust. Set nails and add wood filler to holes. Apply wood conditioner and stain following manufacturer's directions.

6 Hang as desired using appropriate hardware. ✦

KITCHENS

The kitchen is the heart of the home, and if the heart is cluttered, the rest of the house is doomed! Check out these great projects for organizing cookbooks, drawers, countertops and even your favorite snack foods.

SNACK TIME

Design by Theresa Ekdom

Load this dispenser with popcorn packets and keep it next to the microwave. You'll be back in front of the television with your snack before the commercials end!

PROJECT SIZE
7x10¾x5½ inches

TOOLS
- Table saw
- Scroll saw
- Drill with ⁵⁄₆₄-inch bit
- Sander
- Clamps

SUPPLIES
- 1x6 oak: 1 foot
- ½x8-inch oak*: 5 feet
- Wood glue
- Spray adhesive
- Tung oil finish
- Hanging hardware, if desired

*Measurements given are actual, not nominal. Standard nominal lumber will need to be ripped and/or planed to size.

Organizing TIPS

Use a plastic kitchen spatula to protect the surface of the wood when removing a nail. Place the blade of the spatula under the head of the clawhammer as you pry the nail out.

CUTTING

1 From 1x6 oak, use table saw to cut a 7-inch length; rip width to 5 inches (for lid). On the bottom of the lid, mark a line ⁹⁄₁₆ inch from one long and two short edges. Set the table saw blade to a depth of ¼ inch. Cut rabbets on short sides first, ¼ inch deep by ⁹⁄₁₆ inch wide. Cut a rabbet on the long side the same dimensions. This will allow the lid to sit inside the edges of the dispenser.

2 Cut ½-inch-thick oak in two 30-inch pieces. Rip width of one board to 7 inches; rip width of second board to 4½ inches. From 7-inch board cut one 10¾-inch board (for back), and one 7-inch length (for front). From 4½-inch board, cut two 8¼-inch lengths (for sides) and one 6-inch length (for bottom).

3 Transfer back top pattern to top of back piece; cut out with scroll saw.

4 Join front/back pattern pieces as indicated. Make a copy of "popcorn" design; set aside. Transfer line for arched edge onto ½x7x7-inch front piece; cut out with scroll saw.

5 Adhere pattern copy to front using spray adhesive. Cut out design with scroll saw, first drilling a small starter hole in each section to be cut out. For each starburst, insert a No. 2 spiral blade in the hole, then carefully cut each line. Cut each letter using a No. 5 reverse tooth blade. *Note: To keep the sharp points on the lettering, make multiple cuts per letter, coming at each point from both directions from the starter hole (Fig. 1).*

6 Using front pattern, transfer arched edge onto bottom piece, aligning 6-inch straight edge of bottom with dashed line on pattern; cut out with scroll saw.

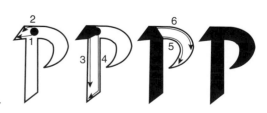

Fig. 1

7 Sand well; remove dust.

ASSEMBLE & FINISH

1 Glue bottom between sides with edges flush. Clamp and let dry.

2 Glue back to sides and bottom with bottom and side edges flush; glue front to sides with top and side edges flush. ***Note:*** *This leaves a slot on the bottom for dispensing the popcorn packets.* Clamp and let dry.

3 Sand surfaces of dispenser; soften edges by sanding, being sure to sand the edges of the slot well. Remove dust.

4 Apply at least three coats of tung oil finish, following manufacturer's directions.

5 Attach hanging hardware, if desired. ✦

Organizing **TIPS**

When choosing small appliances for the kitchen, consider the ones that mount under the cabinets.

Align here for box bottom.

Align here for box bottom.

Left Front/Bottom
Join to right front/bottom for
full-size pattern.

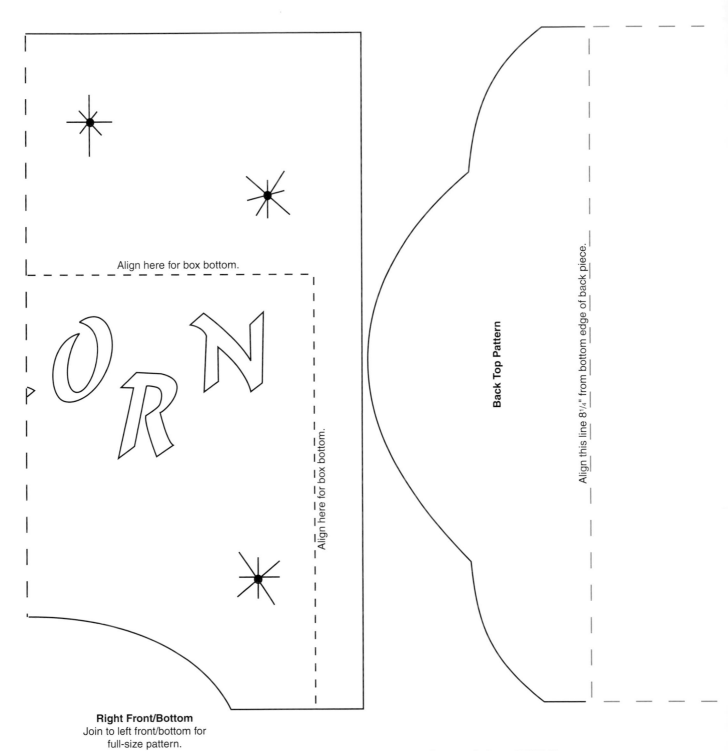

Align here for box bottom.

Align here for box bottom.

Back Top Pattern

Align this line 8¼" from bottom edge of back piece.

Right Front/Bottom
Join to left front/bottom for
full-size pattern.

Organizing **TIPS**
Hang tablecloths on towel racks mounted to the inside of linen closet doors.

SPICE IT UP

Design by Joyce Atwood

Organize those little bottles with an ivy-stenciled cabinet.

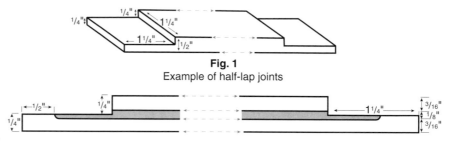

Fig. 1
Example of half-lap joints

Fig. 2
Cut a ⅛"-wide groove
¼" deep, beginning and ending
½" from each end.

CUTTING

1 Referring to cutting diagram, cut two 4½x17-inch pieces (for top and bottom), one 15x17½-inch piece (for back), two 3x15-inch pieces (for shelves), two 3½x17½-inch pieces (for sides), four 1¼x8-inch pieces (for door top and bottom) and four 1¼x17⅜-inch pieces (for door sides).

2 Using router with ¼-inch roundover bit, round both edges on front and sides of 4½x17-inch top and bottom pieces.

3 Using router with ¾-inch straight bit, cut half-lap joints on ends of door top, bottom and side pieces ¼ inch deep by 1¼ inches wide (Fig. 1).

4 To make a groove for the spline which holds the screen in place, use the router with ⅛-inch straight bit to cut a ⅛-inch-wide groove ¼ inch deep across the center of one edge of each door piece, beginning and ending ½ inch from each end (Fig. 2). This will be done most easily on a router table.

ASSEMBLE & FINISH

1 Referring to assembly diagram, glue and nail shelves to back. Apply glue to ends of shelves and side edges of back; nail sides in place flush with back edge, nailing to back and to shelves.

2 Glue and nail top and bottom to back and sides with back edges flush and ½-inch overhang on each end.

PROJECT SIZE
17x18½x4½ inches

TOOLS
- Table saw or radial arm saw
- Router with table and ¼-inch roundover, and ⅛- and ¾-inch straight bits
- Nail set

SUPPLIES
- ½x24x48-inch sheet birch plywood
- Wood glue
- Brads: ½- and 1¼-inch
- Wood putty
- Sandpaper
- DecoArt Americana Satins Primer

and Stain Blocker #DSA34
- DecoArt Americana Satins acrylic paint: sage green #DSA21, light willow #DSA20, dark ecru #DSA06 and hunter green #DSA24
- Paintbrushes
- Ivy stencil
- Stencil brushes
- DecoArt Americana Satins satin varnish #DSA28
- Black fiberglass screen
- Vinyl window spline and spline tool
- Four ½-inch hinges
- Two ¾-inch wooden knobs with screws

3 Fit door pieces together at half laps with edges flush; glue and nail in place.

4 Set nails; fill holes with wood putty. Let dry; sand smooth.

5 Apply primer and stain blocker to all surfaces following manufacturer's directions. Base-coat pieces as follows, applying multiple coats as needed to cover:
Doors, sides and back—*Dark ecru.* Paint both sides of doors. Paint outside only of sides and back. Let dry.
Interior, top, bottom and wooden knobs—*Sage green.* Paint inside of back and sides, both sides of shelves and both sides of top and bottom. Let dry.

6 Dip one end of stencil brush in *hunter green* and the other in *light willow*; stencil ivy pattern around outer edges of doors. Let dry.

7 Apply one or two light coats of satin varnish following manufacturer's directions.

8 Cut screen slightly bigger than openings on doors. Insert edges of screen in door grooves using vinyl window spline and spline tool.

9 Attach doors to sides with ½-inch hinges with outer edges flush. Attach knobs to fronts of doors with screws. ◆

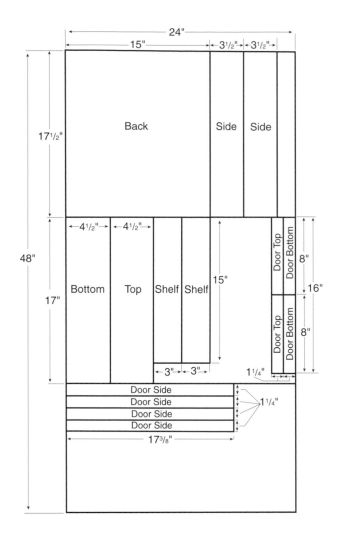

Cutting Diagram

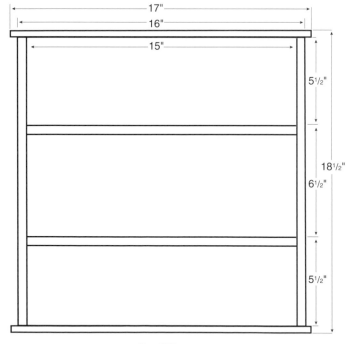

Front View

Assembly Diagram

PATIO
PANACHE

Design by Patti J. Ryan

Enjoy the cool evening breeze as you dine outdoors — a portable caddy holds all the necessary supplies.

PROJECT SIZE
15x30x20 inches, excluding handles

TOOLS
- Table saw or circular saw
- Miter saw
- Drill with ⅛-inch bit and countersink, ¼-inch straight bit and ¾-inch Forstner bit
- Carpenter's square
- Nail set
- Locking pliers

SUPPLIES
- ½-inch birch plywood: 24x36 inches (grain with 24 inches)
- ½x1⅝-inch flat molding: two 7-foot lengths
- 1-inch wood dowel: two 5-foot lengths
- ¾-inch dowel: one 18-inch length
- Single strength acrylic or glass: two 13¾x18¾-inch sheets
- Four double-ended dowel screws
- Six 1½-inch screws
- ¾- and 1-inch brad nails
- Two ¼x1-inch carriage or hex bolts with washers and locking nuts
- Wood glue
- Wood filler
- Sanding block with wet/dry sand-paper: 80-, 180- and 220-grit
- Four ¾-inch furniture gliders
- Tack cloth or damp rag
- 1-inch-square scrap of card stock or paper
- Paper towels or cotton rags
- Paintbrushes: chip brush and high-quality 2-inch brush
- Painter's masking tape
- DecoArt Americana stain conditioner #DSA33
- DecoArt Americana water-based stain: whitewash #AMS10
- DecoArt Americana Satins satin varnish #DSA28
- DecoArt Americana Satins: French blue #DSA43
- 2¼-inch star stamp
- Decocolor opaque white marker
- Four plastic spacer discs

CUTTING

1 Rip ½-inch plywood into two 14x24-inch wide pieces, then cut each to 19-inch lengths for tray bottoms.

2 From each of the 7-foot pieces of flat molding, mitering each end to 45 degrees, cut two 20-inch long point lengths for long sides and two 15-inch long point lengths for short sides. Then with 90-degree cuts and cut two 12-inch lengths for handles.

3 From each 5-foot length of 1-inch dowel, cut two 18-inch lengths for top legs and two 10-inch lengths for bottom legs.

4 Cut the ¾-inch dowel to a 15⅛-inch length for tray handle bar.

5 On the inside of the two long sides of the top tray, measure down ¾ inch at the center and drill ¼ inch deep with a ¾-inch Forstner bit. Drill the rest of the way through with a ¼-inch bit.

6 On one end of each of the handle pieces, mark ¾ inch from the end and centered in the width. Drill a ¾-inch Forstner hole ¼ inch deep and drill the rest of the way through with the ¼-inch bit. On the other end, mark 1 inch from the end and centered in the width and drill a ⅛-inch pilot hole for the 1½-inch screw.

7 Mark the center of each end of each long leg. Predrill one end with a bit slightly smaller than the diameter of the dowel screws, and the other end a ⅛-inch pilot hole for the 1½-inch screws.

8 Mark the center of each end of the short legs. Predrill one end with a bit slightly smaller than the diameter of the dowel screws, and the other end as needed for the furniture gliders.

9 Mark the center of the ¾-inch tray handle dowel and predrill with the ⅛-inch bit.

ASSEMBLY

1 With the bottoms flush, frame both tray bottoms with the long and short sides. Glue and brad-nail into the mitered corners as well as along the outside bottom edges of the sides and into the tray edges. Set the nails and fill with wood filler. Sand flush when dry.

2 With the ¾-inch Forstner holes to the outside, place the tray handle dowel at the opposite end between the handle sides. Secure with 1½-inch countersunk screws (one in each end). Attach the tray handle to the top tray sides with the carriage

bolt and nut, placing the washer between the two pieces of wood. Fill screw heads at dowel end, then sand smooth when dry.

3 Using one of the 1-inch dowels, outline it on a piece of card stock and fold it into quarters to find the exact center. Puncture a pencil hole through the center. Mark this center in each corner of the bottoms of each tray, placing the edges of the dowel template along the inside of the tray sides (See Fig. 1). Drilling from the bottom up, drill ⅛-inch hole in each corner of the top tray, and ¼-inch hole through each corner of the bottom tray.

4 Tap furniture gliders into the appropriately predrilled end of each short leg. Thread one dowel screw into each short leg holding it with the locking pliers. Thread one short leg through the hole in each corner of the bottom shelf.

5 Thread the appropriate end of the long leg onto the dowel screw and tighten. The shelf will be sandwiched between the long and short legs.

6 Place the top shelf over the assembled base and secure with 1½-inch countersunk screws.

FINISH

1 Sand all surfaces with 180-grit sandpaper. Wipe with tack cloth.

2 Apply stain conditioner according to manufacturer's instructions. Lightly sand with 220-grit when dry. Wipe with tack cloth.

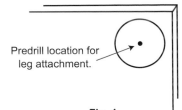

Predrill location for leg attachment.

Fig. 1
Tray Bottom View

3 Apply whitewash stain. Wipe off with soft cloth, let dry for 30 minutes, then recoat. Let dry.

4 Apply satin varnish with high-quality brush. Let dry.

5 Mask off the tray and handle sides except for a 1-inch-wide stripe at the center. Also mask off a 2-inch-wide square in the center of each short side of each tray.

6 With the chip brush, dab the tray sides with *French blue*, following closely with crumpled paper towel, leaving a mottled texture. Let set for a few minutes, then remove painter's tape.

7 Apply paint to stamp and stamp image in 2-inch square on ends of trays. Reload paint each time the stamp is used. Let dry.

8 Apply an additional two coats of satin varnish according to manufacturer's instructions. Let dry and sand with 220-grit sandpaper between coats.

9 Outline star stamp and stripes with opaque white marker.

10 Place plastic spacers over screw heads in top tray and lay acrylic or glass insert into tray. ✦

FESTIVE UTENSIL CADDY

Design by Sandi Hauanio

Inlaid circles add excitement to this spicy kitchen tool holder.

Organizing **TIPS**

Clamp a paperback cookbook onto a wooden pants hanger, then hang over a cupboard doorknob.

PROJECT SIZE
8x8⅝x7¼ inches

TOOLS
- Compass
- Circle cutting jig: up to 7-inch diameter
- Drill with ⅛-inch brad point bit
- Plunge router with ⅛-inch straight and ¼-inch upcut spiral bits
- Table saw with dado blade set
- Combination square
- Clamps: 6
- Straightedge

SUPPLIES
- ½x8¼-inch Baltic birch plywood: one 36-inch length
- Scrap of plywood at least ½x8¼x 27½ inches
- ¼x8-inch yellowheart wood*: one 48-inch length
- ¼x6-inch primavera wood*: one 24-inch length
- ⅛x5-inch padauk*: one 12-inch length
- ½x1-inch padauk:* one 36-inch length
- Double-sided turner's tape
- Wood glue
- 1-inch-wide blue masking tape (painter's tape)
- Cyanoacrylate instant glue with activator
- Sandpaper
- Arm-R-Seal clear satin sealer by General Finishes

Measurements listed are actual, not nominal. Standard nominal lumber will need to be ripped and/or planed to size.

CUTTING

1 Cut the ½x8¼-inch birch plywood base to 27½ inches and place it on the workbench. Begin with the templates about ¾ inch from the edge and place them one after another. ***Note:*** *You will create all four sides of the caddy on this piece of plywood, then cut them apart in a later step.* Mark the centers of the large circles first. Using a compass and referencing the template, draw each circle to its indicated size.

2 Adhere the plywood base to a piece of scrap plywood with double-sided turner's tape and secure the scrap piece to the workbench. Set the depth on the circle cutting jig to ¼ inch. Pilot a pivot hole with the ⅛-inch bit, but don't go all the way through. Adjust the pivot pin to the size of the circle to be cut.

3 Cut circles, adjusting size as you go, until all the circles are cut out from the plywood base. Clean out the circles, taking care not to gouge the outer edges of the circles.

4 Cut the inlaid circles from the ¼-inch yellowheart wood in the following sizes: three 2-inch circles,

two 2¼-inch circles, four 3-inch circles and three 4-inch circles. Secure the yellowheart onto a scrap piece of wood with turner's tape. Predrill a pilot pivot hole and set the router depth to cut all the way through the yellowheart. For each circle needed here, the pivot will actually be set ½ inch bigger than the circle needed—the end result being a perfect fit. Cut all 12 holes. Once all the circles are cut, glue them in place.

Organizing **TIPS**

Screw a cup hook beside the kitchen sink (not over it). Hang jewelry on it while washing dishes.

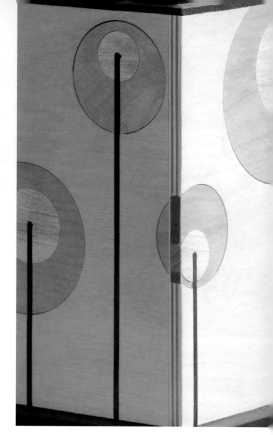

5 Place the template back on the plywood base. Locate and mark the centers of the inner (smaller) circles. Drill the pilot hole only slightly more than ¼ inch deep. Cut out the smaller circles.

6 Cut the primavera circles much like the yellowheart circles. The sizes needed are: four 1-inch circles, five 1½-inch circles, one 2-inch circle and two 2¼-inch circles. Set the pivot to ½-inch bigger than the circle size needed. Glue circles in place as with the yellowheart.

7 Trim off pieces of circles that extend beyond the plywood edges.

8 Place the ⅛-inch router bit in the router. Set depth at ⅛ inch. Check to be sure the plywood is still secure to the work surface. Plunge router into one of the center holes of one of the inner circles. With a straightedge clamped in place as a guide, rout a dado from the circle center to the bottom of the plywood. Repeat for each of the small circle centers.

9 Cut the ⅛-inch padauk into ⅛-inch strips. Glue the strips into the dadoes cut in step 8. Trim off the ends with the table saw.

ASSEMBLE

1 Cut the plywood to size in order and beginning with the first section of the template. Cut section 1 to 6¹³⁄₁₆ inches, section 2 to 5½ inches, section 3 to 6¹³⁄₁₆ inches and section 4 to 5½ inches. When the sides are assembled, the design will appear to wrap around the caddy.

2 With the table saw, cut a ½-inch dado ⁵⁄₁₆ inch deep, beginning ½

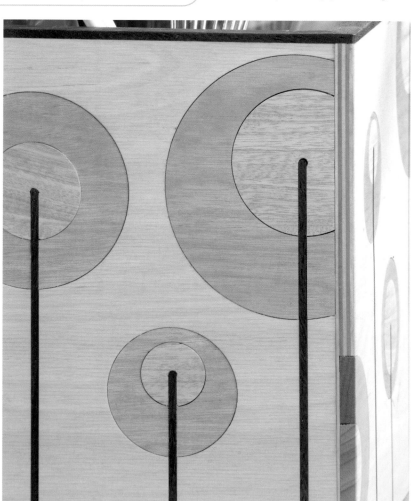

inch up from the bottom of the inside of all four box sides. Cut a rabbet ½ inch wide and ⁵⁄₁₆ inch deep up the vertical sides (both sides) of the 6¹³⁄₁₆-inch front and back.

3 Cut the remaining piece of ½-inch birch plywood to 5½x6⅛ inches for the bottom.

4 Glue and clamp the container together with the bottom in place. Sand.

ACCENT TRIM

1 Cut the remaining ⅛-inch padauk for trim around the top, mitering corners to match.

2 Using the ½x1-inch padauk, miter and cut to fit around the bottom edge of the container.

3 Sand and finish the padauk before attaching it to the box top. Then make sure to keep your hands clean. Glue around top and bottom with cyanoacrylate glue and activator.

FINISH

Note: *As the padauk inherently has a transferring tint, finishing will have to be done in stages.*

1 Tape off the padauk with 1-inch-wide blue painters' tape and finish the body of the utensil holder with clear sealer.

2 When dry, remove the tape from the padauk and tape off the rest of the box. Finish the padauk top and base. ✦

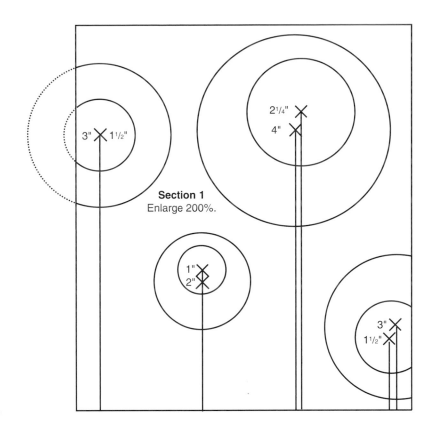

Section 1
Enlarge 200%.

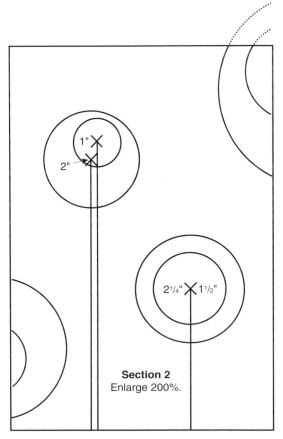

Section 2
Enlarge 200%.

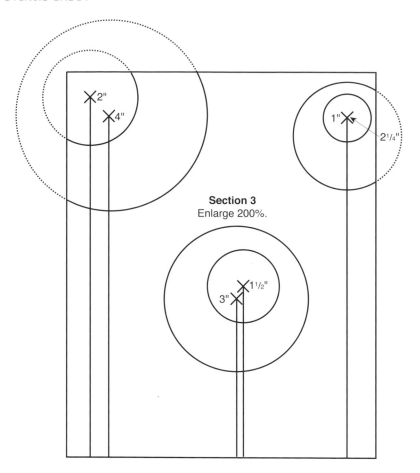

Section 3
Enlarge 200%.

O rganizing **TIPS**

Lost the knobs off of pot lids? An or-
dinary cork will do the trick. Simply
thread a screw through the hole in the
pot lid and screw the cork onto it until
it's tight. It's a great heat-proof knob!

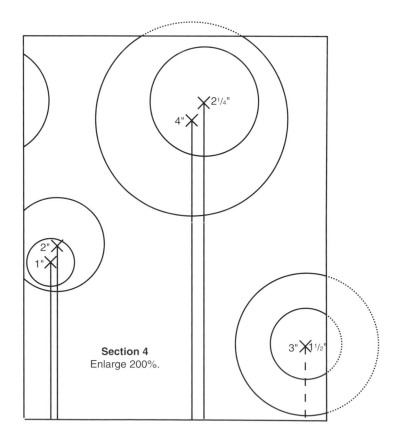

Section 4
Enlarge 200%.

WEATHERED WINDOW MESSAGE CENTER

Design by Anna Thompson

Turn an old window into a message center perfect for use in a kitchen or utility room. Base your cabinet size on that of the old window you use.

PROJECT NOTES

Dimensions in cutting chart are given for model project. The size of cabinet is based on the size of window frame; adjust measurements accordingly.

Remove all glass, tacks and debris from window opening.

Assemble pieces using 1⅝-inch screws, predrilling holes and countersinking screws.

CUTTING

1 Measure height of window frame and subtract ¼ inch. Cut two 1x6s to this measurement for case sides (A).

2 Measure width of window frame and subtract ¼ inch, plus 1½ inches (the thickness of the sides). Cut two 1x6s to this measurement for case top and bottom (B).

3 Cut three 1x4s to same measurement as case top and bottom, for shelves (C).

PROJECT SIZE
14x31x6⅝ inches

TOOLS
- Table saw or band saw
- Carpenter's square
- Drill

SUPPLIES
- Weathered window frame
- 1x6: 8 feet
- 1x4: 4 feet
- 2x4: 18 inches
- Sandpaper
- 1⅝-inch screws
- 2-inch screws
- 3-inch screws
- Acrylic paint
- Satin varnish
- ⅛-inch masonite panel
- Spray-on chalkboard finish
- Cork sheeting
- Spray adhesive
- Glazing points
- Two 2-inch nonmortise hinges

Organizing **TIPS**
The inside of a pantry or closet door is a great place for a message board.

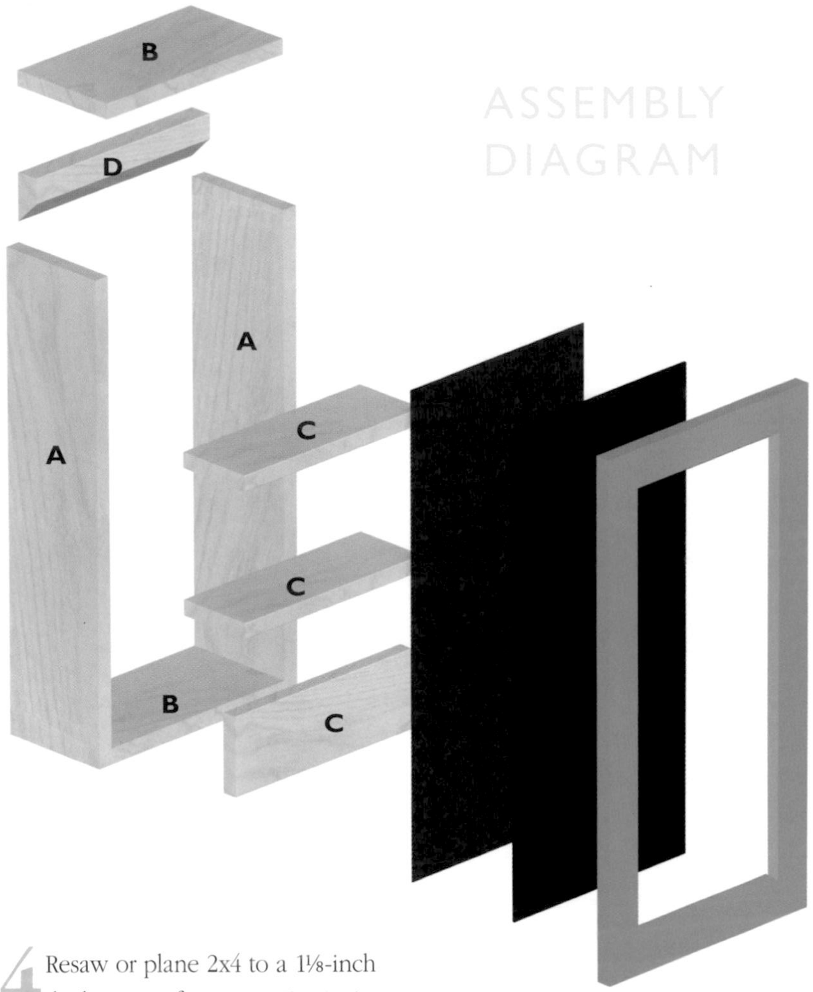

ASSEMBLY
DIAGRAM

(Actual Sizes)

P	T	W	L	#
A	¾"	5½"	23¾"	2
B	¾"	5½"	12¼"	2
C	¾"	3½"	12¼"	3
D	1⅛"	3½"	12¼"	1

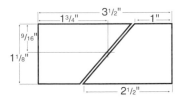

Fig. 1
Hanger Cleat
End View

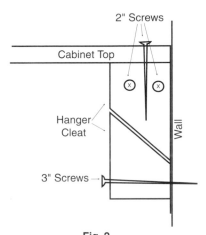

Fig. 2
Side View
Attach one half of hanger cleat
to inside top of cabinet.
Attach remaining half of cleat
to wall.

4 Resaw or plane 2x4 to a 1⅛-inch thickness. Referring to Fig. 1, rip this piece down the middle at a 45-degree angle for hanger cleat (D). Cut both halves to same length as shelves.

5 Sand edges and surfaces smooth.

ASSEMBLE & FINISH

1 Referring to assembly diagram, glue and use 1⅝-inch screws to attach sides (A) to top and bottom (B); check for square.

2 Attach shelves (C) inside case with back edges flush, spacing as desired. ***Note:** Third shelf on model project was attached vertically at bottom for holding phone book.*

3 Attach one half of hanger cleat (D) to inside top of case, flush with back edge, securing on sides and across bottom of cleat with 2-inch screws (Fig. 2).

4 Folllowing manufacturer's directions, paint window frame, case and remaining hanger cleat, then seal with one or two coats of satin varnish.

5 Measure inside opening of window frame (where glass was); cut ⅛-inch masonite panel to these measurements for insert. Spray on chalkboard finish to one side of masonite. Cut cork sheeting to fit

masonite; adhere to opposite side with spray adhesive. Insert in opening and secure with glazing points.

6 Attach hinges on left front side of case 4 inches from top and bottom edges; attach to corresponding positions on window frame.

7 Secure remaining half of hanger cleat to wall using 3-inch screws; hang case so cleats fit together (Fig. 2). ✦

CUTLERY KEEPER

Design by Anna Thompson

Great for flatware in the kitchen or "stuff" anywhere, these organizers will keep every drawer in your home neat and tidy.

PROJECT SIZE
12⅜x2⅛x16¼ inches

TOOLS
- Table saw
- Router with ¼-inch straight bit
- Router table (optional)
- Clamps

SUPPLIES
- ⅜x2⅛-inch wood of choice*: 10 feet
- ¼-inch birch plywood: 12x16
- Wood glue
- ⅝-, 1- and 1¼-inch wire brads
- Sandpaper
- Spray lacquer

*Measurement given is actual, not nominal. Standard nominal lumber will need to be ripped and/or planed to size.

Organizing TIPS
Store cords, brushes and vacuum cleaner attachments in shoebags hung in the closet.

Note: This is a great project for using up scrap pieces of wood.

CUTTING

1 If your wood of choice is 2⅛ inches or wider, rip 5 feet to 2⅛ inches, and 5 feet to 1⅞ inches.

2 On a 5-foot section of the 2⅛-inch width, rout a ¼-inch rabbet ¼ inch deep along the bottom edge.

3 With a 45-degree miter for the box frame, cut the 2⅛-inch stock into: two pieces 16¼ inches long point to long point for sides and two pieces 12⅜ inches long point to long point for front and back.

4 Cut the ¼-inch plywood bottom to 12x15⅞ inches.

5 From 1⅞-inch stock, cut four 11⅝-inch lengths.

ASSEMBLY

1 Glue two sides, top and bottom together, clamp and let dry. Once dry, secure corners with 1¼-inch wire brads.

2 Glue bottom in place and secure with ⅝-inch wire brads.

3 Space three dividers 2⅝ inches apart perpendicular to the fourth divider and secure with glue and 1-inch wire brads.

4 Set divider unit into frame, and glue and secure dividers in place through outside of sides into ends of dividers. Use 1-inch brads.

5 Fill holes, let dry and sand flush.

FINISH

1 Finish with three coats of spray lacquer, sanding between coats. ◆

CHEERY APPLE TOWEL RACK

Design by Barbara Greve

This fun little project is just the thing to hang next to a sink for towels, or in the kitchen for aprons … the possibilities are endless!

Organizing **TIPS**

Hang oven mitts and aprons on peg racks in the kitchen instead of using valuable drawer space.

PROJECT SIZE
17⅛x5⅞x¾ inches, excluding hooks

TOOLS
- Scroll saw
- Miter saw
- Small clamps
- Drill with bit to accommodate screws for hooks

SUPPLIES
- ⅜x20x5⅞-inch beadboard panel with grooves running the 20-inch length
- ⅛x17⅛x5⅞-inch plywood
- ¼x¾-inch screen molding: 48 inches
- ½x1¾-inch scallop molding
- ½x⅝-inch half-round molding: 20 inches
- Eight ¹⁄₁₆x1½-inch Woodsies medium teardrop shapes from Forster
- Fine-grit sandpaper
- Graphite paper
- Americana acrylic paint from DecoArt: antique white #DA58, dark chocolate #DA65, country red #DA18, milk chocolate #DA174, French vanilla #DA184, desert sand #DA77, honey brown #DA163, avocado #DA52 and lamp black #DA67
- Clear gel stain medium
- Wood glue
- Satin varnish
- Two flat metal hooks with screws
- Two 1½-inch sawtooth hangers

CUTTING

1 Rip ⅜-inch beadboard panel to 17⅛x5⅞ inches. From grooved sections of remaining beadboard, cut three ¾x¼-inch lengths for stems.

2 Miter screen molding at corners to fit around beadboard with outer edges flush.

3 Cut scallop molding in half and place pieces side-by-side with flat edges together and scallop edges mirroring each other; position patterns for left and right apples on scallop molding and cut as shown in Fig. 1.

4 Cut five pieces of half-round molding 3 inches long. Referring to center apple pattern, cut 45-degree angles at the top and bottom of two pieces.

5 Glue two teardrop shapes together to make four ⅛-inch-thick leaves; clamp together until dry.

6 Sand all rough edges.

ASSEMBLE & FINISH

1 Glue beadboard panel on top of plywood with edges flush; clamp until dry. Glue and clamp screen molding around beadboard panel; let dry.

2 Paint fronts and sides with acrylic paint as follows, letting dry after each coat:

Rack—Base-coat frame with *desert sand*, then *dark chocolate*. Base-coat bead-board with *French vanilla*. Mix equal parts *honey brown* and clear gel stain medium; paint over beadboard, wiping with paper towel to achieve antique effect.

Left and right apples—Base-coat with *dark chocolate*, then *antique white*. Use graphite paper to transfer detail; paint peelings *country red* and seeds *lamp black*.

Center apple—Base-coat molding strips with *dark chocolate*, then *antique white*, then *country red*.

Leaves—Basecoat with *dark chocolate*, then *antique white*, then *avocado*.

Stems—Base-coat with *milk chocolate*, then *dark chocolate*.

3 Lightly sand painted pieces to distress.

4 Position left and right apples on beadboard 1½ inches from the inside of the frame and ½ inch from bottom; position center apple between left and right apples. Lightly sand areas on rack where apples are placed, for better adhesion; glue apples in place. Using photo as a guide, glue stems and leaves at tops of apples, first sanding rack lightly as for apples.

5 Apply two coats of satin varnish to rack following manufacturer's directions.

6 On back, drill a hole ⅜ inch from bottom edge and 5½ inches from each side; secure metal hooks with screws in predrilled holes. Attach saw-tooth hangers at top for hanging. ◆

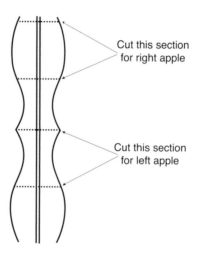

Cut this section for right apple

Cut this section for left apple

Fig. 1
Place scallop molding pieces side-by-side
with flat edges together and scallop edges mirroring each other.
Cut across molding pieces in four places, as shown.

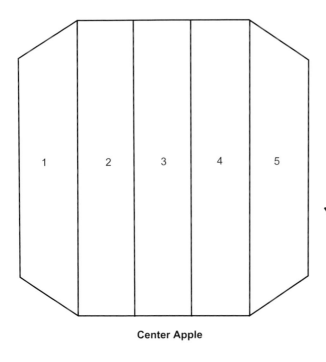

| 1 | 2 | 3 | 4 | 5 |

Center Apple

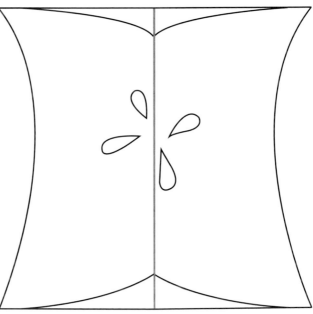

Left Apple

Right Apple

Organizing **TIPS**

Screw a cup hook beside the kitchen sink (not over it). Hang jewelry on it while washing dishes.

NOW YOU'RE COOKING

Design by Loretta Mateik

Your cookbook collection will have room to grow with this expandable book rack.

Note: Cut the dowel rods to suit your needs. For this project, the rack will expand to approximately 16 inches.

CUTTING

1 Cut ½-inch plywood into two 8-inch lengths. Cut dowels into four 18-inch lengths.

2 Copy side template onto tracing paper, then transfer pattern onto side pieces. Round three edges on each side piece (as indicated in pattern) with router and ⅛-inch roundover bit.

3 Drill holes with ½-inch Forstner bit.

PAINTING

1 Basecoat all pieces with *burnt sienna*. Let dry, then sand all surfaces, remove dust and recoat.

2 Finish all pieces with matte spray finish/sealer.

ASSEMBLY

1 Check the fit of the ½-inch dowels. If too snug, widen the hole with the mini sander (Dremel with sanding bit used here). Wipe clean.

2 Slide dowels into rack; add cookbooks. ✦

PROJECT SIZE
18x6x8 inches

TOOLS
- Table saw
- Router with ⅛-inch roundover bit
- Drill with ½-inch Forstner bit
- Mini sander (or Dremel tool with sanding bit)

SUPPLIES
- ½-inch birch plywood: 6x18 inches
- ½-inch wooden dowel: 6 feet
- Tracing paper
- Transfer paper
- DecoArt Americana acrylic paint: burnt sienna #DA63
- Paintbrushes
- Sandpaper
- DecoArt Americana matte spray finish/sealer #DAS13

RECIPE TREASURY

Betty Crocker's PICTURE COOK BOOK

Currint

Stonecroft Family
COOKBOOK

Ston
COO

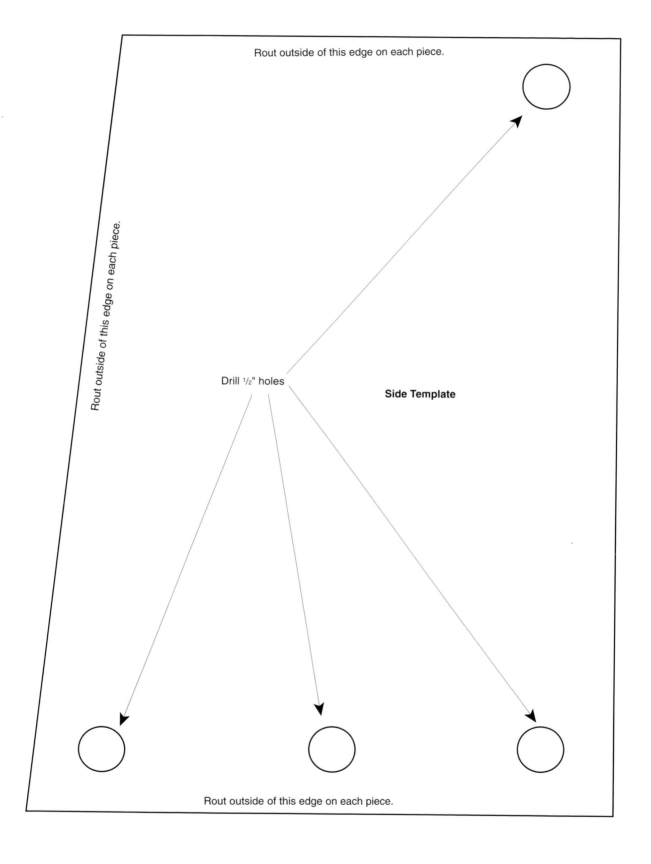

Rout outside of this edge on each piece.

Rout outside of this edge on each piece.

Drill ¹/₂" holes

Side Template

Rout outside of this edge on each piece.

WINE GLASS HOLDER

Design by Delores Ruzicka

Add elegance to an easy project with a purchased stencil.

PROJECT SIZE
28¼x8x11¼ inches

TOOLS
- Jigsaw
- Palm sander
- Drill

SUPPLIES
- 1x12 pine: 3 feet
- 1x8 pine: 3 feet
- Sandpaper
- Graphite paper
- DecoArt Americana Satins: soft natural #DSA40 and Victorian plum #DSA15
- DecoArt Americana acrylic paint: sable brown #DA61, black forest green #DA83, shale green #DA152, Hauser light green #DA131, summer lilac #DA189, primary red #DA199, burgundy wine #DA78, bright orange #DA228 and titanium white #DA01 and burgundy wine #DA022
- Paintbrushes: ¾ wash and #6 flat
- American Traditional bountiful fruit border overlay stencil #CD-017
- Stencil brushes
- Spatter brush
- Four 2-inch screws

Organizing TIPS
Use a clean dustpan (that you keep just for this purpose!) to transfer chopped veggies to a skillet or wok.

PROJECT NOTES
When painting, apply multiple coats as needed to cover, letting dry after each coat.

Base-coating may raise the grain of the wood. If so, sand all pieces lightly and wipe clean before applying second coat.

CUTTING
1 Cut 1x12 pine to 28¼-inch length for glass holder. Use graphite paper to transfer slot pattern four times across board as indicated on pattern. Cut slots using jigsaw with a fine blade. Sand smooth.

2 Cut 1x8 pine to 28¼-inch length for back. Transfer rounded corner pattern to each top corner and cut out with jigsaw. Sand smooth.

FINISH & ASSEMBLE
1 Base-coat glass holder with *Victorian plum*. Base-coat back with *soft natural*.

2 **Note:** *Stencil half of back at a time. When first half is completed and dry, flip stencil to finish second half of back.* Find center of back. Position stencil beginning at center point and use stencil brush to fill in as follows:

Grapes—*Summer lilac*; shade with *Victorian plum* and highlight with *titanium white*.

Apples—*Primary red*; shade with *burgundy wine* and highlight with *titanium white*.

Leaves—*Shale green* and *Hauser light green*; shade with *black forest green*.

Peaches—*Peach*; shade with *bright orange*.

3 With #6 flat brush, apply *sable brown* shading around leaves and fruit; let dry. Use spatter brush to spatter back with *sable brown.* Let dry.

4 Place back on top of glass holder with side and back edges flush. Attach with 2-inch screws through bottom of glass holder. Hang as desired with appropriate hardware. ✦

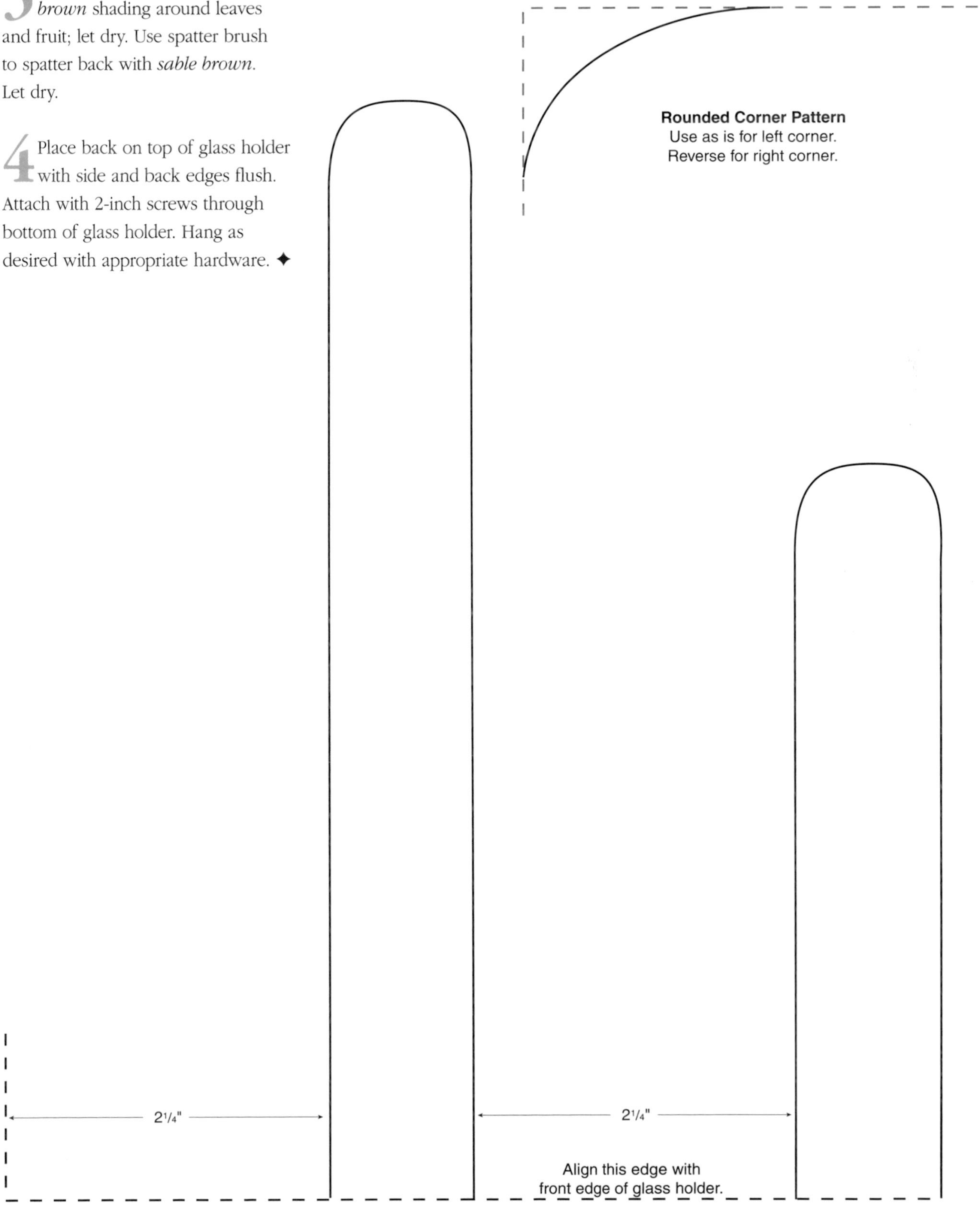

Rounded Corner Pattern
Use as is for left corner.
Reverse for right corner.

2¹⁄₄"

2¹⁄₄"

Align this edge with
front edge of glass holder.

Slot Pattern
Transfer pattern four
times across glass holder.

HOBBY AREAS

Hobby areas are notoriously cluttered with pieces and parts from projects in various stages of completion. Find projects here for woodworkers, crafters, quilters and more!

CRAFTY ROLL-AROUND

Design by Anna Thompson

Scrapbook papers, rubber stamps and all manner of creative supplies find a home in this versatile little unit.

CUTTING

1 Cut the ½-inch plywood following the cutting diagram. The result will be two ½x14x23⅞-inch pieces for top (C) and bottom (D), two ½x14x15⅞-inch pieces for sides (A) and two ½x9⅞x22¹³⁄₁₆-inch pieces for use in step 2.

2 Maintaining the length, rip the 22¹³⁄₁₆-inch boards from step 1 to 5 inches wide (R), 4 inches wide (Q), 3⅞ inches wide (P) and 2⅞ inches wide (O) as shown on cutting chart. These are the drawer faces.

3 Rout rabbets ¼-inch deep and ¼-inch wide in the back edges of both sides (A), the top (C) and the bottom (D).

4 Dry-fit the case together. Measure the rabbeted opening in the back and cut the back (E) from the ¼-inch birch to 23⅜x16⅜ inches. Adjust these measurements if necessary for a nice fit.

5 Rip the 1x4 cherry (or other hardwood) into six ½-inch-wide drawer runners (B), then cut them to 13¼ inches.

DRAWER BOX

1 Plane (or have planed) the 1x6 pine boards to ½ inch thick.

2 Rip the first board to 2¾ inches, the second board to 3⅛ inches, the third board to 3⅜ inches and the fourth board to 4⅝ inches.

3 Lower the table saw blade to ¼ inch and set the fence ½ inch away from the closest edge of the blade. Make one pass with each of the ½ inch boards from steps 1 and 2 of the drawer box. Reset the fence

PROJECT SIZE
24x20⅜x14¾ inches

TOOLS
- Table saw or circular saw
- Router with ⅜-rabbet or straight bit
- Planer
- Sanding block
- Drill or cordless screwdriver
- Nail gun (optional)

SUPPLIES
- ½-inch veneer core cherry or birch plywood: 2x8 feet
- 1x4 cherry (or other hardwood): one 2-foot length
- 1x6 clear white pine: four 6-foot lengths
- ¼-inch birch plywood: 4x4 feet
- Cherry (or birch) iron-on edge tape: 39 feet
- ⅝- and 1¼-inch brad nails
- Sandpaper
- Glue
- Turner's tape or double-sided carpet tape
- Sixteen ¾-inch screws
- Eight 1-inch drawer knobs
- Two 5-inch handles
- Four 2½-inch wheels
- Sixteen ½-inch screws to mount wheels

⅝-inches from the near side of the blade. With the same edge against the fence, make another pass with each ½-inch board. This should result in a ¼-inch-wide and ¼-inch-deep groove for the drawer bottom the length of each board.

4 Cut each board to two pieces 13 inches long for the sides (F, H, J and L) and two pieces 21⅞ inches long for the front and back (G, I, K and M).

Note: *Clamp a "stop block" to the bed of your saw when you have multiple cuts of the same length. This allows all the pieces to be exactly the same measurement.*

5 From the ¼-inch birch plywood, cut four pieces 22¼x12½ inches for the drawer bottoms (N).

CASE ASSEMBLY

1 Iron on the veneer edging to all four edges of the top and bottom, the front and back only of the sides, and all four edges of each drawer front (O, P, Q, R). Rub down with a sanding block and 220-grit sandpaper.

2 Attach the ½x¾-inch drawer runners (B) to sides (A). Predrill through the ¾-inch width, then glue and screw into the side. Measure from the top, and place end of the runner flush with the inside of the rabbet, and the top of a runner at each of the following marks: 2⅞ inches, 6⅝ inches, and 10⅝ inches. Repeat with the second side.

3 Glue and nail the case together with 1¼-inch nails. The sides (A)

will butt into the top (C) and bottom (D). Make sure the rabbet is to the inside and back on all boards during assembly.

4 Glue and nail the back (E) in place with ⅝-inch brad nails.

DRAWER ASSEMBLY

1 Assemble the top drawer box by butting the back (G) into the sides (F), then gluing and nailing in place with 1¼-inch brad nails. Slide the bottom (N) in place, then attach the front (G) with glue and nails.

2 Attach top drawer cherry face (O) to drawer box, flush at the bottom, by securing with double-sided tape. Slide into position in the case, check for fit, then secure with four

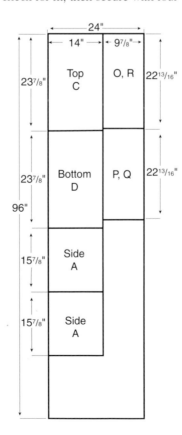

Cutting Diagram

¾-inch screws predrilled and driven in from the inside of the box.

3 Assemble bottom drawer and face as above using parts L, M, N and R. Slide both the top and bottom drawers in place.

4 Build the two middle boxes: second drawer using H, I and N; third using J, K and N. Place double-sided tape on the box front of each drawer and slide into respective slots in case.

5 Place drawer face P in place on the second drawer and face Q on the third drawer. This will allow for perfect placement of the faces on the two middle drawers. Remove from the case, still taped to respective drawer boxes, and attach with four ¾-inch screws in each drawer.

FINISH

1 Finish as desired. This model was kept natural to show off the beauty of this wood.

2 Install drawer knobs 3½ inches in from each end of the drawer and centered on the width of the drawer face.

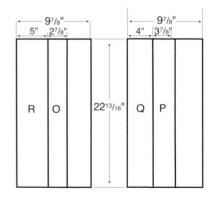

Cutting Drawer Faces

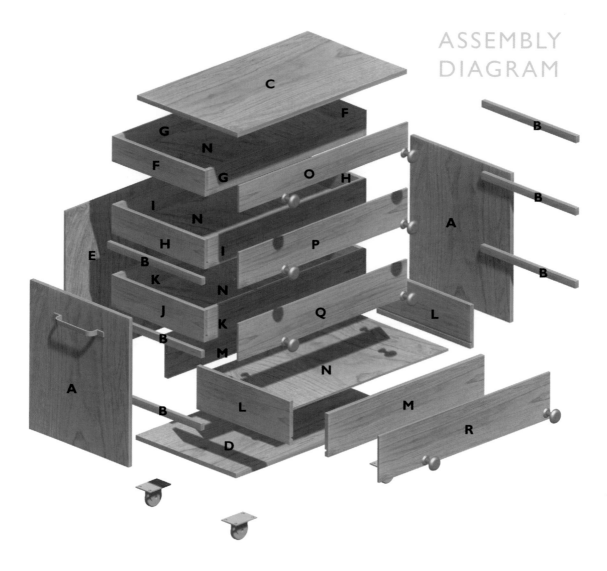

CRAFTY ROLL-AROUND
(Actual Sizes)

P	T	W	L	#
A	½"	14"	15⅞"	2
B	¾"	½"	13¼"	6
C	½"	14"	23⅞"	1
D	½"	14"	23⅞"	1
E	¼"	23⅜"	16⅜"	1
F	½"	2¾"	13"	2
G	½"	2¾"	21⅞"	2
H	½"	3⅛"	13"	2
I	½"	3⅛"	21⅞"	2
J	½"	3⅜"	13"	2
K	½"	3⅜"	21⅞"	2
L	½"	4⅝"	13"	2
M	½"	4⅝"	21⅞"	2
N	¼"	22¼"	12½"	4
O	¼"	2⅞"	22¹³⁄₁₆"	1
P	¼"	3⅞"	22¹³⁄₁₆"	1
Q	¼"	4"	22¹³⁄₁₆"	1
R	¼"	5"	22¹³⁄₁₆"	1

3 Attach handles to each side 4 inches down from the unit top, and centered side to side.

4 Attach 2½-inch rollers in the four corners with ½-inch screws. ◆

RIBBON RAINBOW

Design by Loretta Mateik

Keep spools of craft ribbons neat and tidy on this handy wall organizer.

CUTTING

1 Cut 1x6 to one 24-inch length for back, then plane the remainder to ½ inch thickness. Cut the ½-inch board to two 6-inch lengths for the sides.

2 Copy side template onto tracing paper with stylus, then transfer pattern onto side pieces. Round corners with scroll or jigsaw; drill holes for dowels with ⅜-inch Forstner bit; and pilot screw holes near side bottom with ⅛-inch straight bit.

3 Cut ⅜-inch dowel to 27½-inch lengths. Measuring ½ inch in from each end of each dowel, drill a %₄-inch hole all the way through the dowel.

PAINTING

1 Base-coat all pieces with *Williamsburg blue*. Let dry, then sand all surfaces with mini sander or sandpaper; remove dust and recoat.

2 Finish all pieces with matte spray finish/sealer.

ASSEMBLE

1 Check the fit of the ⅜-inch dowels. If too snug, widen the hole with the mini sander. Wipe clean.

2 Attach sides to back with 1¼-inch countersunk screws.

3 Attach appropriate hardware and hang rack on wall.

4 Slide dowels into rack, adding ribbon spools.

5 Insert small pieces of ⅛-inch dowel into holes in end of ⅜-inch dowels to prevent rod from sliding out. (20 gauge wire bent into "T" pins may be substituted for the ⅛-inch dowel here.) ◆

PROJECT SIZE
25x5½x6 inches

TOOLS
- Table saw
- Planer
- Scroll saw or jigsaw
- Drill with ⅛- and %₄-inch straight, countersink and ⅜-inch Forstner bits
- Mini detail sander (Dremel)

SUPPLIES
- 1x6 pine: one 4-foot length
- ⅜-inch wood dowel: one 5-foot or two 30-inch lengths
- ⅛-inch wood dowel (optional: 20 gauge wire)
- Tracing paper
- Transfer paper
- DecoArt Americana acrylic paint: Williamsburg blue #DA40
- Brushes for painting
- Sandpaper
- 1¼-inch drywall screws
- DecoArt Americana matte finish/spray #DSA13
- Hardware to hang

Organizing **TIPS**

Bungee cords stretched between wall studs create storage space in a garage or basement for shovels, rakes, skis or any oddly shaped item.

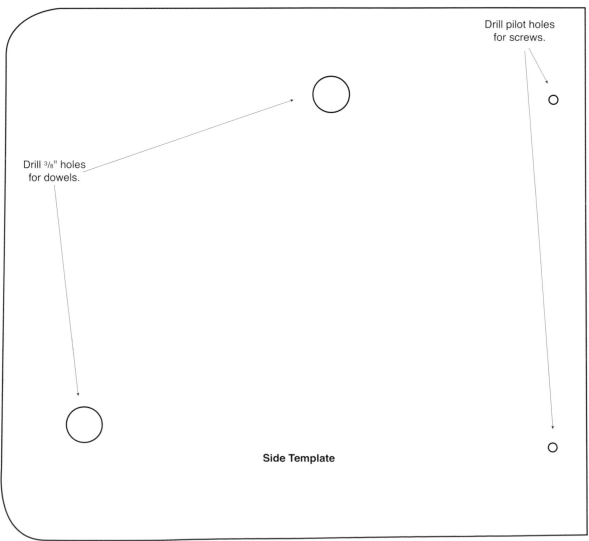

Drill pilot holes for screws.

Drill ³/₈" holes for dowels.

Side Template

READY FOR ACTION

Design by Bev Shenefield

Keep sports equipment, outdoor games or garden supplies in a sturdy storage bench made of car siding.

PROJECT NOTE

When you build this project, be sure the surface you are working on is level.

CUTTING

1 Cut the 2x3 pine into four 34½-inch pieces for frame front and back (A); four 21½-inch pieces for frame sides (B); six 12¼-inch pieces for frame uprights (C) and four 2½-inch pieces for feet (E).

2 Inspect the car siding you have on hand. From the nicest boards, cut four lengths to 36¼ inches and set aside for the top (H).

3 From the rest of the car siding, cut twelve 24-inch lengths for front and back (F); six 36-inch lengths for the sides (G); and six 24½-inch lengths of car siding for bottom (D). These are all oversized so if a piece is an inch or so short, it will still be usable. These will all be cut to fit in later steps.

FRAME

1 Assemble frame by screwing through the 1½-inch side of the front and back pieces (A) and into the frame sides (B) with 2½-inch screws. Build two identical frames. Both should measure 34½x24½ inches.

2 Add frame uprights (C) at the corners with top of upright flush with top of frame. Predrill down through the top of the frame about 1 inch with ⅜-inch bit, then drive one 2½-inch screw into the upright from each side of the frame front and back (A) and frame sides (B). Repeat at all four corners.

3 On the bottoms of the front and back top rails, measure and mark 17¼ inches from the side. Center an upright at each of these marks and attach as in the previous step.

PROJECT SIZE
36¼x20¼x26 inches

TOOLS

- Table saw
- Drill with ⅛- and ⅜-inch bits
- Framing square
- Miter saw
- Straightedge
- Level
- Router with ⅜-inch roundover and V-groove bits

SUPPLIES

- 2x3 pine: four 8-foot lengths
- P116 (car) siding: eleven 8-foot lengths
- 1¼-, 2-, 2½- and 3-inch screws
- Four 3-inch galvanized or electro-coated screws
- Exterior-grade wood glue
- Wood filler
- Sandpaper
- Clear polyurethane finish
- Brushes
- Two 2½-inch butt hinges
- One or two lid supports

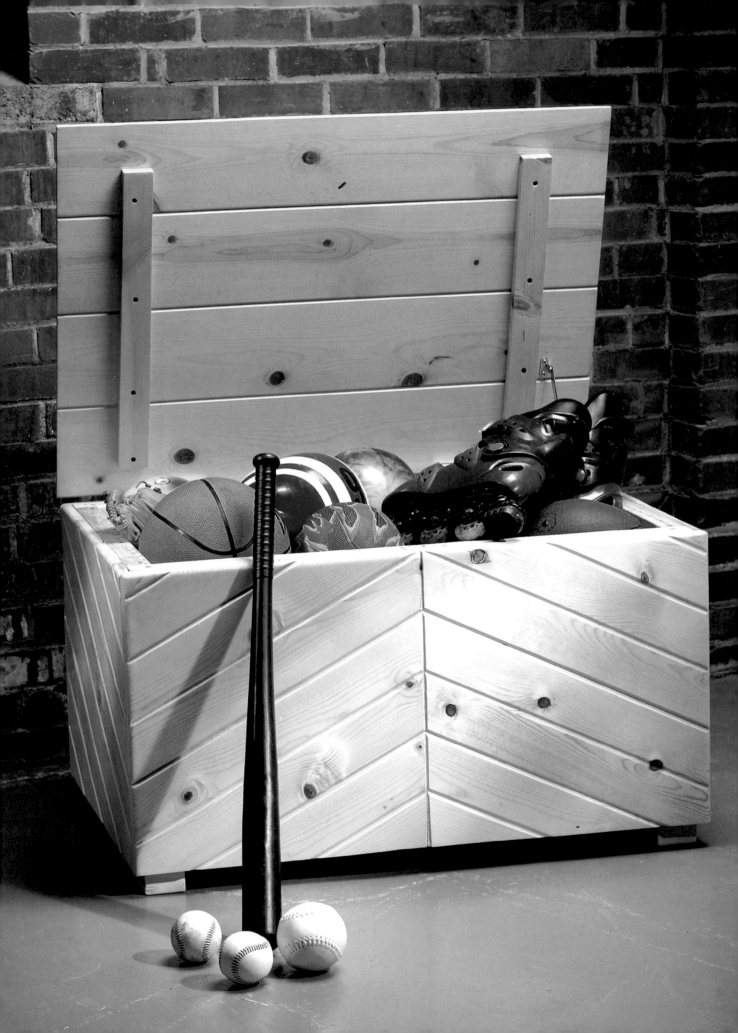

4 Turn unit upside down and attach bottom frame with bottom of upright flush with bottom of frame.

5 Set the table saw fence to 4¾ inches. With the tongue of the car siding against the fence, rip one of the bottom pieces (D). Place this piece on the bottom frame first with the sides and the ripped edge flush with the frame. Tack in place with two 2-inch screws driven through the car siding and into the frame. Dry-fit the remaining bottom car siding pieces across bottom of frame. Mark the overhang on the end piece and rip it on the table saw with the groove end against the fence. Be sure the saw blade passes on the side of the line that is waste. (This should be about 4¼ inches.)

Note: When fastening the bottom in place, you have the option of the grooves facing up or down. On this model they are down, for a smoother "floor" inside. You may also prefer to use galvanized screws when securing the floor, especially if the bench has the possibility of being exposed to moisture (like dew-covered grass).

6 Glue bottom pieces in place and secure with 2-inch screws.

7 Set one foot piece (E) in each corner and secure to bottom with glue and one galvanized or electro-coated 3-inch screw. Predrill the hole with ⅛-inch bit. Be sure to drive this into the frame, and not just through the floor. Lightly sand over the edges of the foot bottoms.

FRONT SIDING
Note: You may choose to run the

siding level instead of at an angle as this model is. If so, just measure from side to side and cut the siding to length. Make the front and back long enough to cover the side edges.

1 Set the box up so it is resting on its back. From the center mark on the front top rail, use a square to mark the center of the upright down the whole length. This is the center reference line — both sides (left and right) of the front panels will meet

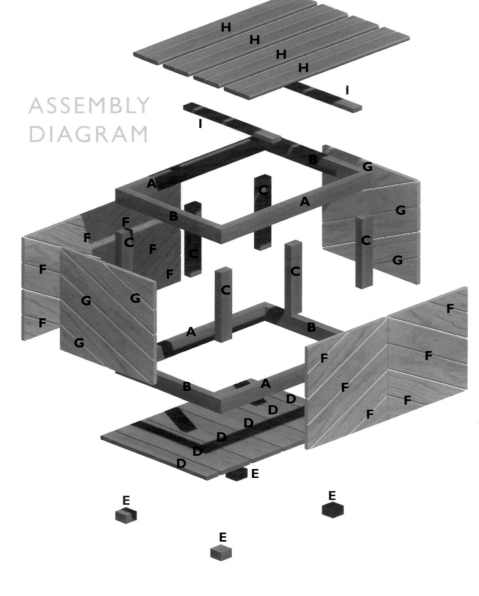

ASSEMBLY DIAGRAM

READY FOR ACTION
(Actual Sizes)

P	T	W	L	#
A	1½"	2½"	34½"	4
B	1½"	2½"	21½"	4
C	1½"	2½"	12¼"	6
D	¾"	7"	24½"	6
E	1½"	2½"	2½"	4
F	¾"	7"	24"	12
G	¾"	7"	36"	6
H	¾"	7"	36¼"	4
I	¾"	2"	20½"	2

here. Measure down on the front side of each corner and mark 8⅝ inches. (Extend this line around the corner to the sides.) Draw a line with the straightedge or square, from the top front center mark to the front corner mark, both to the left and to the right. This is your siding angle.

2 Temporarily screw the pieces left from ripping the bottom onto each side flush at the front for spacers. Cut a 6/12 angle (see sidebar on page 103) on one 24-inch front piece (F) so the long point is at the tongue. Place it on the face with the bottom lined up to the angle line, and the angle just cut even with the center line. Evaluate the fit: Is there room to add a piece above it and below it without creating teensy corner pieces? See how it looks with the tongue on the line, or with the center groove on the line. Choose which layout you like, mark the back of the board at the top frame and again at the edge of the spacer. Cut these angles, then place it back on the face of the box and see how it fits. It should be flush with the side (with spacer) and the top. It should also be square along the vertical centerline. **Option:** *You may wish to fasten a straight scrap piece of wood along the centerline opposite the side you are beginning with. This will give you a solid surface to "butt into" at the center. Temporarily secure this piece with 2-inch screws driven into it from the inside of the case. Cut the 6/12 angle in each board first (three will be mirror images of the other three for left and right sides), then continue to set, mark and cut siding until that side of the front is filled. The last bottom piece and the last top piece should come*

out of the same piece of wood. Secure all the pieces in place with glue on the frame and the tongue and 2-inch screws driven from the inside out through the top, bottom and center frames or 3-inch screws at corners. Be careful to avoid driving a screw through at the "V" groove. Remove glue runs as they occur.

3 Repeat the process for the opposite side, matching the grooves for the second half to the first half.

SIDE SIDING

1 Remove the spacers from the sides. Measure from the front (including the siding) toward the back 18 inches and mark the top of the side frames. Draw a line from that mark on each side to the 8⅝-inch mark coming around from the front. This is now your angle reference line for the sides.

2 Mark, cut and install side pieces (G) as you did the front siding. This time the long point for the 6/12 angle will be at the groove end of the car siding. Where the front started in the middle and went down to the corner, the side will match grooves at the corner and go up toward the top. Try to create a nice tight fit as the side pieces butt into the front. Secure with glue and 2-inch screws driven from the inside of the box out and into the back of the siding. Remove glue runs as they occur.

3 Repeat this process until both sides are "sided."

BACK SIDING

Square the centerline down the center upright of the back. Draw the

reference line from the middle top of the back to 8⅝ inches down on each side. The "flow" of the back will be as though the siding just wrapped around the corner and kept going up. Work with one side of the back at a time fitting each piece (F) between the sides and the centerline. Remove glue runs as they occur.

TOP

1 Dry-fit the four top boards (H) together. Center from side to side, then examine what needs to be trimmed off of the front and back. Mark each board, then trim as desired. Assemble back together, gluing the tongues. Remove glue runs as they occur.

2 From pieces of scrap siding, create two lid supports (I) 2 inches wide and 20½ inches long. Place them 4 inches in from each side and 4 inches from the back edge. Secure to lid bottom with glue and one 1¼-inch screw into each top piece, avoiding the center and the groove.

FINAL MILLING

1 With the ⅜-inch roundover bit, rout the sides and front of the top and the top edges and all four corners of the box.

2 Change bits to the "V" groove bit. Set it to ¼-inch depth. Clamp a straightedge to the front so the point of the "V" groove will go right down the center of the front where the two front sections join. Do the same on the back.

3 Fill any areas necessary with wood filler. When dry, sand the surface of the entire unit.

FINISH

1 Remove dust and seal with three coats of clear polyurethane, lightly sanding between coats.

2 Install hinges beginning 7¾ inches in from each edge.

3 Install lid support. ✦

Cutting a 6/12 angle

To draw a 6/12 angle, take a look at your framing square. (This is a very versatile tool that can be used to determine and cut rafters and stair treads, but here, we just want to make a consistent angle on several pieces of wood.) Notice that there are inch lines on the inside and outside of both the 1½- and the 2-inch sides. A 6/12 angle means you place the square on your wood so the 12-inch mark is along the edge.

Then, while holding the square in place at the 12-inch mark, slide the square up or down until the other side is at the 6-inch mark. For this to work properly, however, if you use the inside 12-inch mark on the 2-inch side, you must use the inside 6 inch mark on the 1½-inch side. Inside to outside, or outside to inside won't give the angle you want. It must be inside to inside or outside to outside. See angle/pitch drawing.

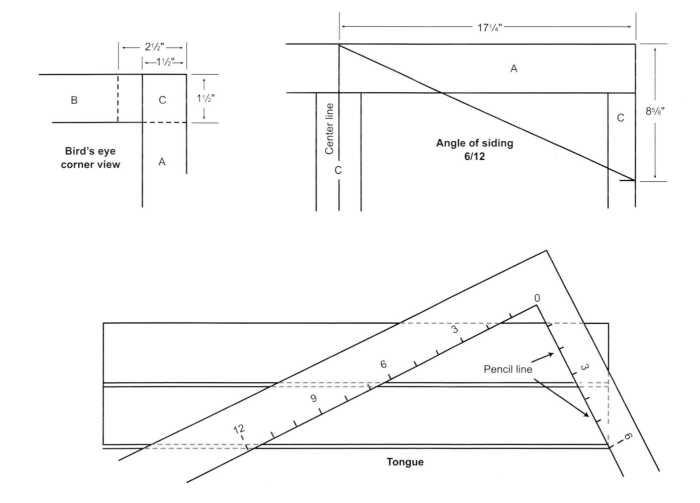

Bird's eye corner view

Angle of siding 6/12

Tongue

Pencil line

IT'S A WRAP

Design by Patti J. Ryan

You'll never have to search for paper or tape again when you store wrapping supplies in this portable caddy.

CUTTING

1 Cut and label ½-inch plywood according to cutting chart.

2 Cut the ⅜-inch dowels to five 30¼-inch lengths for wrapping paper holders and the ¼-inch dowels to two 10½-inch lengths for ribbon holders.

3 Referring to rod hole placement diagram (page 106), mark placement of holes on inside of both side pieces at 1½, 3⅝, 5⅞, 8⅛, 10⅜ and 14½ inches from top. On inside of left side only, make additional marks on front edge ½, 2⅝, 4⅞, 7⅛, 9⅜ and 13½ inches from top; draw lines connecting each mark on front edge with center mark.

4 Using ¾-inch Forstner bit, drill ¼-inch-deep holes at each center mark on both side pieces; drill a hole in the center of each vertical divider.

5 Using router with ½-inch straight bit, rout marked slanting lines on left side ¼ inch deep. **Note**: *Use straightedge as a guide to keep lines straight.*

6 Mark 1 inch down from the top of the door and centered side to side. Drill a 1-inch finger hole at this mark.

7 Sand all drilled holes and slots.

ASSEMBLE

1 Glue sides to top and bottom and secure with 1¼-inch drywall screws. Predrill and countersink holes through the top and bottom and

PROJECT SIZE
32x18x6⅛ inches

TOOLS
- Table saw or circular saw
- Router with ½-inch straight bit
- Drill with #6 countersink bit and ⅛-inch pilot bit, and ¾- and 1-inch Forstner bits
- Carpenter's square
- Straight edge

SUPPLIES
- ½-inch birch plywood: 3x3 feet
- ⅛-inch Luaun or finish plywood: 2x3 feet
- ⅜-inch dowel rods: five 3-foot lengths
- ¼-inch dowel rods: one 2-foot length
- Transfer paper
- Twenty-two 1¼-inch drywall screws
- Small brads
- Wood glue
- Wood filler
- Sanding block: 180- and 220-grit wet/dry sandpaper
- Tack cloth (or damp rag)
- Paintbrushes: chip brush and quality 2-inch brush
- Paper towels or cotton rags
- DecoArt Americana chestnut #AMS03 water-based stain
- DecoArt Americana stain conditioner #DSA33
- DecoArt Americana Satins satin varnish #DSA28
- 1½- or 2-inch hinges: 2
- Magnetic door latch
- 4-inch handle

into the top and bottom of the sides. Check for square.

2 Mark 10 and 10½ inches from each end of the center shelf. Place shelf next to the bottom of the box so ½ inch of the bottom extends past the shelf at both ends and draw identical lines across both pieces. Place the vertical dividers at these lines, making sure the divider with the slot is in position with the side with no slots.

3 Set shelf in place and secure through the sides with glue and countersunk 1¼-inch screws. Glue and secure vertical dividers to shelf with countersunk 1¼-inch screws. Secure the bottom of the vertical dividers through the frame bottom.

4 Trial fit the door; trim if necessary.

5 Trial fit all dowels in place and trim if necessary.

6 Measure the back of the frame and cut ⅛-inch Luaun to fit (approximately 18x32 inches).

FINISH

1 Cover all screw heads with wood filler. Sand flush when dry.

2 Sand all surfaces with 180-grit sandpaper. Wipe with tack cloth or damp rag.

3 With chip brush, apply stain conditioner to all wood surfaces and let dry.

4 Sand with 220-grit sandpaper, then wipe with tack cloth or damp rag.

5 Stain with chestnut stain and wipe off with paper towel or rag. Let dry at least 30 minutes.

6 Apply at least two coats of satin varnish with quality 2-inch brush, sanding with 220-grit sandpaper between coats.

FINAL ASSEMBLY

1 Attach back to frame with brad nails.

2 Install hinges to the bottom face edge of the door beginning 1 inch in from each edge. *Note: Use ½-inch or smaller screws to attach hinge to door.*

3 Attach magnetic catch inside the top edge of the door and door frame.

4 Center the handle on the top of the frame and attach — predrill for screws. *Optional: If preferred, mount gift wrap caddy on wall using appropriate hardware.* ◆

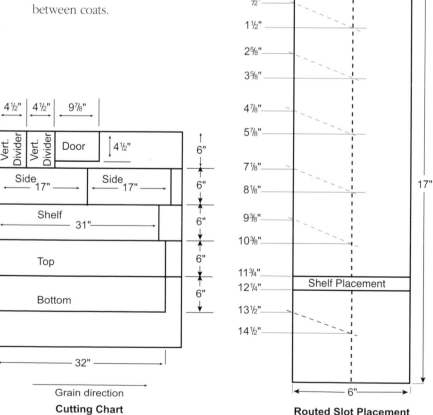

Cutting Chart

Routed Slot Placement

STAIRWAY STORAGE

Design by Bev Shenefield

Turn the black hole under the basement stairs into a shining example of "a place for everything and everything in its place."

PROJECT NOTES
Determining the angle of your stairway is a much simpler process than it sounds. Take a 2-foot square and a 2-foot level (or even a torpedo level) to your stairway. You may need an extra set of hands, so have a friend or family member help you. Place the square against the stairway and line up the outside bottom edge of the square with the stair slope at the 12-inch mark. Have your help hold the square so that end does not move from that point. Place the level along the bottom of the square and move the corner up or down until it is level (See Determining Pitch diagram, page 111.) Now take note of where the outside vertical edge of the square is. For this model, the vertical number was 10¼. That means that for every 12 inches of horizontal run, it rises 10¼ inches. This is called a "ten and a quarter twelve" pitch.

PROJECT SIZE
36x60¾x24 inches

TOOLS
- 2-foot square
- 2-foot level
- Circular saw
- 4-foot straightedge
- Drill with ⅜-inch bit
- Tri-square or protractor
- 36–40-inch bar clamps
- Router with ⅜-inch rabbeting bit
- Brad nailer with ⅝-, 1- and 1¼-inch brad nails
- Random orbit sander

SUPPLIES
- 2x4 pine: 10 feet
- ¾-inch birch plywood: one 4x8 sheet
- ¾-inch birch plywood: one 2x8 sheet
- ¼-inch birch plywood: one 4x8 sheet
- 1x4 hardwood (hidden support): 3 feet
- Colonial doorstop: 20 feet
- 36–48 inch scrap wood: 2
- ¼x½-inch screen molding: 20 feet
- 2¼ inch modern (or colonial) base: 4 feet
- ⅝-, 1- and 1¼-inch nails
- 1⅝- and 3-inch drywall screws: 8 each
- Wood glue
- Natural wood filler
- Sandpaper
- 2½-inch casters: 4
- 1½-inch #10 screws: 16

CUTTING
Note: Label pieces as they are cut for ease of assembly later.

1 Cut the 2x4 into two pieces 34½ inches (A) and two pieces 16½ inches (B).

1 With the 2x4s flat, make the base frame attaching the two side pieces (B) to the front/back pieces (A) by drilling halfway through the 3½-inch width of the front and back with the ⅜-inch bit and securing with 3-inch screws. See Bottom Frame Assembly on page 111.

2 Place ¾x23½x34½-inch bottom shelf (C) on frame. Make sure sides and corners match. Adjust if necessary. Glue and nail in place with 1¼-inch brad nails.

3 Set the base up on what will be its face and place the tall side (66 inches) and short side (30 inches) in place, flush at the bottom and the front, and clamp the sides there. Take the 36–40-inch scrap piece of wood and tack it to one of the uprights, hook your measuring tape onto that upright and measure 36 inches—outside to outside. Tack the other end of the scrap wood into this upright so the space stays the same. Measure up from the bottom of the long side and mark 58½ inches. The height you use for this side is determined by the height of the stairway where this unit will be placed. Using the principles learned about pitch determination: This is a 3-foot-wide unit, so if the tall side is 58½ inches and the drop is 10¼ inches for each foot, the short side will be 30¾ inches shorter, or 27¾ inches. Measure from the bottom of the short side and mark 27¾ inches. With the 4-foot straightedge as a guide, draw a line across the edge of each piece of ¾-inch plywood between these marks. Unclamp the sides from the base. Use the reference

2 Cut ¾-inch birch plywood according to the cutting diagram. Label each piece as indicated.

3 Cut the 1x4 hardwood to 34½ inches then rip into three 1-inch strips for front shelf supports (G).

4 Cut six pieces of colonial doorstop 22½ inches for shelf supports (F).

5 From colonial doorstop, cut two 34½-inch pieces for front shelf trim (I).

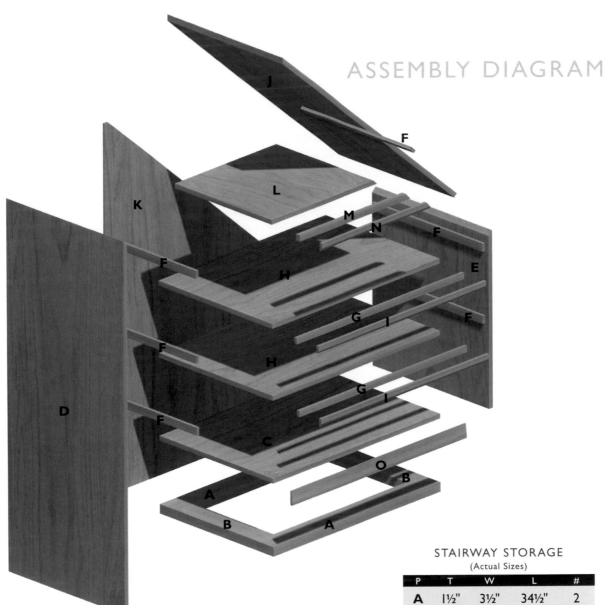

marks to determine the angles of the cuts for the side pieces and the top piece using a tri-square or protractor.

Note: *Experiment with scrap wood to get the correct angles and to have them fit properly together. It may save you lots of wasted material later.*

4 Draw a line all the way across the tall side (D) at the 58½-inch mark. This is the long point measurement. Cut the angle so the inside of the tall side will be shorter as you follow the cut line. Set the circular saw to 43 degrees. Clamp a straightedge onto the side to use as a saw guide to assure the cut stays straight. See Angled Cuts diagram.

5 With the saw still set at the 43-degree angle, cut one end of the rough-cut 52-inch top piece (J).

6 Set the saw to 47 degrees, measure from the long point at the top of the top board (J) and make a mark at 46¼ inches. Square across for a cut line. Clamp a straightedge onto the side to use as a saw guide to assure the cut stays straight. Cut the angle again with the cut line being

STAIRWAY STORAGE
(Actual Sizes)

P	T	W	L	#
A	1½"	3½"	34½"	2
B	1½"	3½"	16½"	2
C	¾"	23½"	34½"	1
D	¾"	23¾"	58½"	1
E	¾"	23¾"	27¾"	1
F	½"	1¼"	22½"	6
G	¾"	1"	34½"	3
H	¾"	23½"	34½"	2
I	½"	1¼"	34½"	2
J	¾"	23¾"	46¼"	1
K	¼"	35¼"	57"	1
L	¾"	23½"	20"	1
M	¾"	1"	20¼"	1
N	½"	1¼"	20½"	1
O	⅜"	2¼"	36"	1

the long point. The long points should be on the same side (top side) of the board, and the short points should be on the same side (inside).

7 Draw a line all the way across the short side (E) at the 27¾-inch mark. Clamp a straight edge onto the side to use as a saw guide to assure the cut stays straight. With the blade set back to 90 degrees, cut the short side to length.

8 With the router deck resting on the inside back of each piece, rout a rabbet ¼ inch wide by ⅜ inch deep in the inside back of each side (D) and (E) and the top (J).

SHELF PREP

1 Attach a ¾x1x34½-inch shelf front support (G) to the bottom of the first shelf (H) with glue and 1⅝-inch screws. Set it ½ inch back from the front edge of the shelf. See shelf detail drawing.

2 Glue and nail a 34½-inch long colonial doorstop (I) in front of the front shelf support with 1-inch brad nails.

3 Repeat steps 1 and 2 for the other 34½-inch shelf.

ASSEMBLE

Note: *Always check for and immediately wipe off any glue runs.*

1 Glue and nail the tall side to the base frame flush at the front and bottom. Attach the short side the same way. Space the sides with the scrap piece of wood as before. Tack the second scrap piece of wood to the

bottom of the short side, and move it up as an angle brace to the long side. Check the corners for square and tack the scrap wood to the long side to maintain square.

2 Dry-fit the top piece to see if any adjustments need to be made. Remove. It will be assembled in a later step.

3 Measure up from the top of the base shelf and mark both sides at 12 and 24¾ inches, then also mark the tall side at 37½ inches. Square lines across for shelf support locations. Glue and nail five of the shelf supports (F) as marked, with the back edge of the support flush with the inside edge of the back dado, using ⅝-inch nails. The sixth shelf support will be placed later.

4 Set the two middle shelves in place and secure with glue and 1¼-inch brad nails through the outside of the side and into the ends of the shelves. Shelves should be flush with the edge of the back dado, and flush with the front.

5 Glue and nail top (J) in place with 1¼-inch brad nails.

6 Measure the width between rabbets, then the height from the bottom of the base to the top of the rabbet on the long side, and from the bottom of the base to the top of the rabbet on the short side. Cut the back (K) from the ¼-inch plywood. Pull off the braces.

7 Glue and nail the back (K) in place with ⅝-inch brad nails. Secure into two middle shelves and around the edges.

TOP SHELF

1 Cut a scrap piece of wood to 12 inches. Stand this piece on end on the top of the middle shelf and butt its side against a tri-square. Slide along the shelf until it touches the bottom of the angled top. Mark that point and square it front to back and onto the ¾-inch face edge.

2 Measure from the tall side at the shelf support to the line just drawn. This is the long point measurement of the top shelf (L). Mark the 26½-inch plywood to that length (approximately 20 inches), then cut at a 43-degree angle with the long point at the bottom.

3 Test-fit the top shelf (L). With the square end resting on the shelf support, the angled end should rest with the bottom edge (long point) right on the line. If all is well, use the 12-inch scrap wood for a prop and glue and nail the shelf in place.

4 Trim the back top corner of the last 22½-inch colonial doorstop and nail it under the top shelf into the top with ⅝-inch brad nails.

5 Hold the last piece of front shelf support (M) against the tall side at the bottom of the shelf and mark the angle. Cut on the miter saw.

6 Cut the same angle on a piece of colonial doorstop (N), then cut it to length.

7 Install the ¾-inch front shelf support (M) to the shelf as before. Nail the colonial doorstop in place flush with the face of the shelf.

FINISH TRIM

1 Measure the width of the front base. Cut the modern casing to 36 inches for piece (O). Glue and nail it flush to the top of the base shelf.

2 Band the entire face of the unit (front edges of the short and tall sides, the top and all three shelves)

with the ¼x½-inch screen mold. Use glue and ⅝-inch brad nails.

3 Fill all nail holes with natural wood filler. Let dry.

4 Sand the entire unit. Sand down all filled nail holes as well as any sharp corners — especially at the tops

of the sides.

FINISH

1 Seal with three coats of clear polyurethane.

2 Install casters with #10 1½-inch screws. ✦

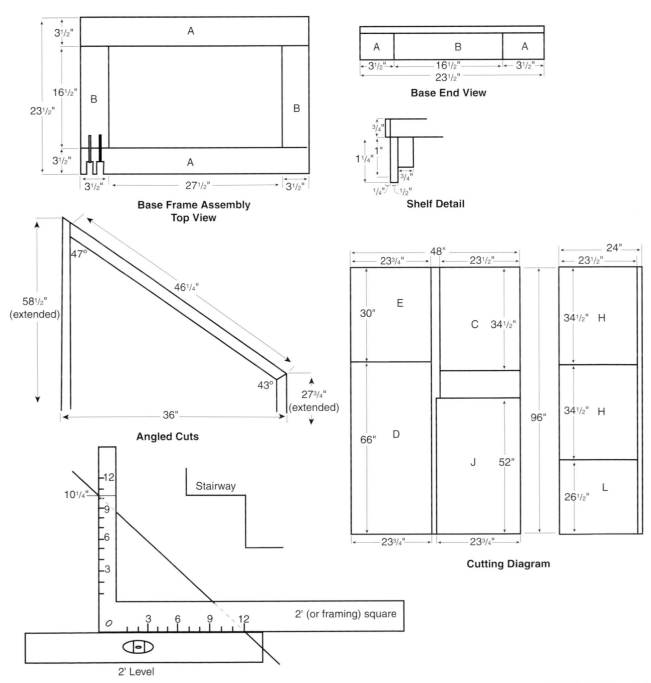

Base Frame Assembly Top View

Base End View

Shelf Detail

Angled Cuts

Determining Pitch

Cutting Diagram

GRANDMA'S SEWING BOX

Design by Anna Thompson

Recreate those fond memories of yesteryear with a vintage-look place to store supplies.

CUTTING

1 Plane the 1x8 to ½-inch thickness, then rip three full lengths at 2-inch width.

2 With the table saw, cut a dado along the bottom of this 2-inch stock ¼ inch wide and ¼ inch deep beginning ⅛ inch up from the bottom edge.

3 With the miter saw set at 45 degrees, cut the following with both ends mitered for the drawer frames: cut ten 7⅝-inch lengths for box sides; two 16¾-inch lengths for bottom front and back; and eight 8¼-inch lengths for four movable drawers front and back.

4 From the ¼-inch plywood, cut four pieces 7x7⅝ inches for the movable drawer bottoms, and one piece 7x16⅛ inches for the stationary bottom.

5 Rip the poplar into 1-inch strips, then cut two pieces 11¾ for handle sides and one piece 7¾ inches for handle top.

6 Referring to handle detail, shape handles with the band saw, cutting the inside away ¼ inch. Sand cut edges smooth.

7 Rip 1x10 to 8 inches, then cut into two 8½-inch lengths for lid.

8 Cut ¼x½-inch oak into four 7¾-inch lengths and eight 4¼-inch lengths for oak hinges. Round corners with band saw.

ASSEMBLE & FINISH

1 Glue together the four movable boxes using two 8¼-inch front and back, two 7⅝-inch side pieces

---

PROJECT SIZE
17x11¾x9¼ inches

TOOLS
- Planer
- Table saw
- Miter saw
- Scroll saw or band saw
- Drill with ¼-inch bit and ⅜-inch countersink bit

SUPPLIES
- 1x8-inch pine: one 6-foot length (drawer frames)
- ¼-inch birch plywood: 24x24 inches
- 1x10-inch pine: 24 inches (lid)
- ¾x4-inch poplar*: 36 inches (handle)
- ¼x½-inch oak*: 6 feet
- Twenty-eight ¼x1-inch machine screws with washers and cap nuts
- Wood glue
- Two 1½-inch hinges
- Six 1-inch drywall screws
- Six ⅜-inch plugs
- Sandpaper
- Desired paint
- Spray lacquer sealer
- Two 5-inch handles

Measurement given is actual, not nominal. Standard nominal lumber will need to be ripped and/or planed to size.

and one 7x7⅝-inch bottom piece for each drawer.

2 Glue together the stationary box with two 16¾-inch front and back, the two remaining 7⅝-inch sides, and the 7x16⅛-inch bottom.

3 Paint unit with your color of choice then seal with spray lacquer.

4 Attach handle sides to handle top with glue and countersunk 1-inch screws. Plug holes with ⅜-inch plugs. Sand smooth.

5 Place movable boxes on top of stationary ones with the ends flush. Mark locations of holes to be drilled for machine screws (see placement drawing). Drill with ¼-inch bit.

Organizing TIPS

Tack a length of elastic to the inside of your cosmetic drawer to keep small tubes from sliding around and tipping over.

6 Drill holes in oak hinges to match holes in shelves, then attach with machine screws and cap nuts. Make sure a washer is placed between the oak hinges and the drawer body.

7 Attach handle base in center of stationary shelf and up from the bottom ⅛ inch.

8 Install 5-inch handles to sides of top movable drawers and 1½-inch hinges to connect lid. (These hinges should be mortised.) ✦

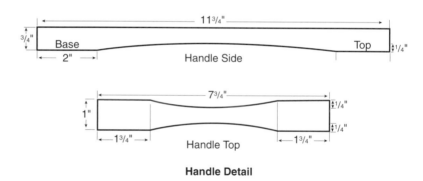

Handle Detail

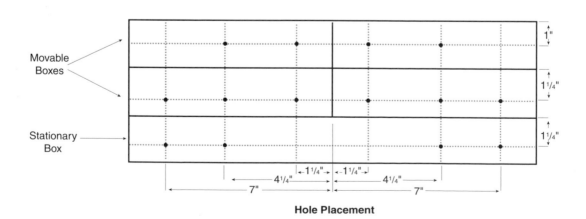

Hole Placement

CRAFTER'S BONANZA

Design by Bev Shenefield

Craft supplies are notorious for expanding to fill any available space. Keep your supplies organized and easy to find with this cabinet.

Note: Each section of the frame is cut and assembled individually (see frame assembly diagram). All four sections are then assembled to complete the frame.

CUTTING FRAME ENDS

1 Set the table saw fence to cut a width of 1¼ inches; make one pass with each of two 6-foot 1x4 boards.

2 Turn the leftover piece of each board over so the factory edge is against the fence and rip them again. There should now be six 6-foot lengths: four ¾x1¼-inch boards and two ¾x¾-inch boards (actual measurements).

3 From the ¾x1¼-inch boards, use the miter saw to cut four 31¼-inch posts (A) and four 19½-inch end rails (B). From the ¾x¾-inch boards, cut four 20½-inch end shelf supports (C).

ASSEMBLE FRAME ENDS

1 Measuring from the bottom of two posts (A), mark 17¾ and 25½ inches. Butt an end rail (B) between the two posts with the top at the 17¾-inch mark. Secure each end of the end rail in place by driving a 2-inch screw through the post into the rail. Attach a second end rail (B) in same manner at the 25½-inch mark.

2 Place the rail/post assembly flat on the work surface. Center one end shelf support (C) on top of each rail/post (support will be ¾ inch short at each end). Drop the support (C) ½ inch below the top of the rail; attach with glue and 1¼-inch screws or brad nails (Fig. 1).

3 Repeat steps 1 and 2 to assemble the second frame end.

CUTTING FRAME FRONT

1 Set the table saw fence to cut a width of 1¼ inches; make one pass with each of two 8-foot 1x4 boards.

2 Turn the leftover piece of each board over so the factory edge is against the fence and rip them again. There should now be six 6-foot lengths: four ¾x1¼-inch boards and two ¾x¾-inch boards (actual measurements).

3 From the ¾x1¼-inch boards, use the miter saw to cut three more 31¼-inch posts (A) and four 33⅜-inch rails (D). From the ¾x¾-inch boards, cut two 69-inch front/back shelf supports (E).

ASSEMBLE FRAME FRONT

1 Measuring from the bottom of each of the three posts (A), mark 17¾ and 25½ inches. Butt a rail between two of the posts with the top at the 17¾-inch mark. Secure each end of the rail in place by driving a 2-inch screw through the post into the rail. Attach a second rail in the same manner at the 25½-inch marks.

2 Butt the remaining two rails against the remaining post and secure with 2-inch screws driven in from the outside, then secure the loose ends of the rails to the center post either with screws or 2-inch finish nails.

3 Lay the front assembly flat on the work surface. Center a front/back shelf support (E) across each rail/post (support will be ¾ inch short at each

---

PROJECT SIZE
72x40x25 inches

TOOLS
- Table saw
- Drill with ⅛- and ¼-inch bits
- 2-foot square (or framing square)
- Brad nailer with ¾-inch brad nails
- Jigsaw
- Router with ¼-inch roundover bit

SUPPLIES
- 2x4 pine: one 12-foot length
- 1x4 #2 white pine: four 6-foot and three 8-foot lengths
- ½-inch plywood: one 2x6-foot sheet
- ½-inch plywood: one 4x6-foot sheet*
- ¼-inch plywood: two 4x8-foot sheets
- 1¼-, 1⅝-, 2- and 3-inch drywall screws
- ⅝-, 1¼-inch nails
- Primer
- Paint to match countertop
- Paint brushes and rollers
- 72-inch preformed countertop with caps

Since only 6 feet is needed from one sheet of ½-inch plywood, it may be less expensive to purchase a whole sheet rather than pay the per-square-foot price.

ASSEMBLY DIAGRAM

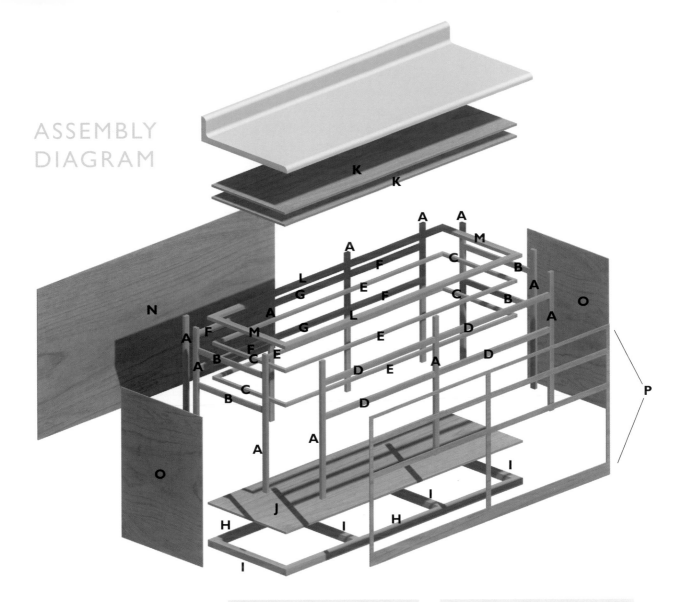

	CRAFTER'S BONANZA			
	(Actual Sizes)			
P	**T**	**W**	**L**	**#**
A	¾"	1¼"	31¼"	11
B	¾"	1¼"	19½"	4
C	¾"	¾"	20½"	4
D	¾"	1¼"	33⅜"	4
E	¾"	¾"	69"	4
F	¾"	1¼"	22"	4
G	¾"	1¼"	21½"	2
H	1½"	1⅝"	70½"	2
I	1½"	1⅝"	20¼"	4
J	½"	23½"	70½"	1
K	½"	22"	69"	2
L	¾"	1¹¹⁄₁₆"	70½"	2
M	¾"	1¹¹⁄₁₆"	20⅛"	2
N	¼"	34"	70½"	1
O	¼"	34"	23¾"	2
P	¼"	34"	71"	1

end). Drop the support ½ inch below the top of the rail and secure in place with glue and 1¼-inch screws or brad nails.

CUTTING FRAME BACK

1 Set the table saw fence to cut a width of 1¼ inches; make one pass with each of two 6-foot 1x4 boards.

2 Turn the leftover piece of each board over so the factory edge is against the fence and rip them again. There should now be six 6-foot lengths: four ¾x1¼-inch boards and two ¾x¾-inch boards (actual measurements).

3 From the ¾x1¼-inch boards, use the miter saw to cut four more 31¼-inch posts (A), four 22-inch back rails (F) and two 21½-inch back rails (G). From the ¾x¾-inch boards, cut two more 69-inch front/back shelf supports (E).

ASSEMBLE FRAME BACK

1 Measuring from the bottom of the four posts (A) mark 17¾ and 25½ inches. Butt a 22-inch back rail

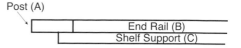

(F) between two posts with the top at the 17¾-inch mark. Secure each end of the rail in place by driving a 2-inch screw through the post into the rail. Attach a second back rail (F) in same manner at the 25½-inch mark. Repeat with two more posts (A) and two more 22-inch back rails (F) to make two identical sets.

2 Butt the two 21½-inch rails (G) between the two sets of frame back post/rail assemblies and secure the rails to the center posts either with screws or 2-inch finish nails.

3 Lay the back assembly flat on the work surface. Center a front/back shelf support (F) across each rail/post (support will be ¾ inch short at each end). Drop the support ½ inch below the top of the rail and secure in place with glue and 1¼-inch screws or brad nails.

ASSEMBLE FRAME UNITS

1 Butt one of the frame end assemblies into the end of the frame back assembly with edges flush. Secure with several 2-inch screws driven from the outside of the frame back corner posts into the frame end posts.

2 Attach remaining frame end to frame back in same manner, then attach frame front to frame ends, butting frame ends into frame front.

Note: At this point, the frame will feel like it is rather flimsy. Be patient. It will become sturdier. When the project is finished, you will be glad the frame is this light!

CUT & ASSEMBLE BASE

1 Cut the 12-foot 2x4 board into 6-foot and 4-foot lengths.

2 Set the table saw to rip a width of 1⅝ inches; make one pass with each board, then turn the factory edges against the fence and make a second pass. There should now be two 6-foot boards, each 1½x1⅝ inches, and two 4-foot boards, each 1½x1⅝ inches (actual measurements).

3 Cut the two 72-inch boards into two 70½-inch lengths for base front/backs (H), and the two 48-inch boards into four 20¼-inch lengths for base supports (I).

4 Lay out the two 70½-inch base front/back boards (H), and place the four 20¼-inch base supports (I) between them, one flush at each end and two evenly spaced in the middle. Attach front/backs to supports with 3-inch screws through the outside of the front/back supports. Make sure the tops are flush.

FRAME UNIT FLOOR

1 From the 4x6-foot ½-inch plywood, cut a piece 23½x70½ inches for floor (J).

2 Turn the assembled frame unit upside down and rest it on the tops of the posts. Place the floor upside down on top of the frame unit (which is now the bottom) and attach it to the frame unit with one 1⅝-inch screw driven into each of the 11 posts.

3 Place the base on the floor; spread construction adhesive on top of the base, then turn the frame unit and

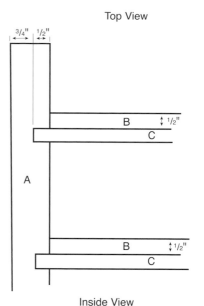

Fig. 1
Drop the support (C)
½" below the rail (B):
so that top of shelf (K)
will sit flush with top of rail (B).

floor right-side-up on top of the base; secure with 1¼-inch nails or screws.

SHELVES

1 From the remaining ½-inch plywood, cut two 22x69-inch pieces for shelves (K).

2 By working at an angle, place the first shelf on the lower shelf supports; nail in place with 1¼-inch nails. Place the top shelf in place on the upper shelf supports and nail in place.

3 Cut the 8-foot 1x4 board into one 70½- and one 20¼-inch length.

4 Check the table saw fence—it should still be set for a 1⅝-inch width. If not, adjust to that width. Rip each board, then turn the remaining piece so the factory edge is against the fence and rip again.

5 Glue and nail the 70½-inch front/back top caps (L) between the end frames, flush with top edges.

6 Glue and nail the 20¼-inch end top caps (M) into the tops of the end posts and at an angle into the front/back caps (L).

Note: The top cap allows for a good surface from which to secure the countertop.

ENCLOSING

1 Measure the back and cut one piece of ¼-inch plywood to fit (N). (It should measure about 34x70½). Temporarily tack back in place.

2 Measure for each side. Cut one side (O) from the remainder of the sheet from which the back was cut, and the other side (O) from another

sheet of plywood. (These should measure 34x23¾ inches.) Glue and nail sides in place, nailing into the base, the posts, the rails and the top frame.

3 Measure and cut the face sheet (P) and temporarily tack it in place. (It should measure about 34x71 inches.) Pull the back off. Reach through and mark the openings with a pencil. Glue and nail the back in place.

4 Remove the face; cut the openings in the face sheet with the jigsaw, then glue and nail the face in place. *Note: Do not cut right to the lines, but leave ¼–⅛ inch.*

5 Roundover the openings and the front corners with the router and ¼-inch roundover bit.

6 Predrill several ¼-inch holes, angled in slightly, down through the top cap. *Note: These are pilot holes to be used in fastening the countertop in place.*

FINISH

1 Fill nail holes, then sand the unit to prep for painting.

2 Apply primer to entire unit, then paint with two coats of paint.

3 Set countertop on the unit so back is flush with the back of the unit and there is ½-inch overhang on each side. Fasten with 2-inch screws driven into the bottom of the countertop through the pilot holes. ◆

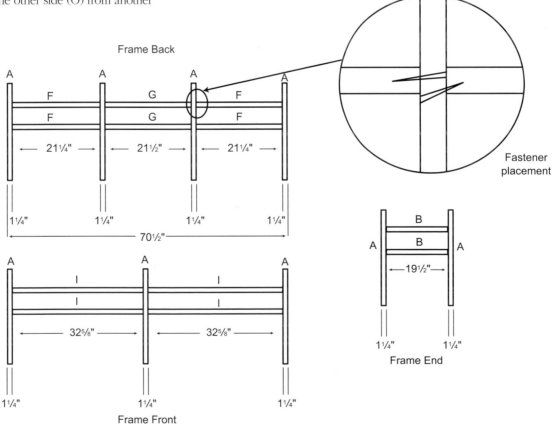

Frame Assembly Diagram

TIMELESS
TOOL CADDY

Design by Kate Langan

Size this caddy to fit your favorite Japanese saw, or make it
bigger or smaller as you wish.

PROJECT NOTES

Be careful of drill angles so screws do not protrude through the bottom or sides of the caddy.

Construction of this piece could be done with hand tools if preferred, using a coping saw to cut the curves and hand planes to cut the bevels and dado.

CUTTING

1 From ½ inch pine, using table saw cut two sides 20⅛x4¾, one handle piece 20⅝x6½ and two end pieces 9½x4¾.

2 From ⅝-inch pine board, cut a 17-inch length (for bottom).

3 Set miter gauge on table saw at 70 degrees; recut ends of sides and handle at this angle.

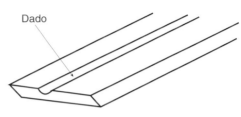

Fig. 1
Cut a 70° bevel on ends of bottom and on bottoms of ends.

Fig. 3
Cut a ½"-wide by ³/₁₆"-deep dado down the center of bottom piece.

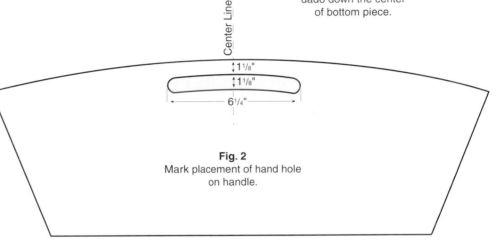

Fig. 2
Mark placement of hand hole on handle.

4 Referring to Fig. 1, tilt the table saw blade to cut the bevels on the bottoms of the end pieces and the two ends of the bottom panel. Mark the center lines of each piece.

5 Stack the two side pieces and center the batten along the top edge. Spring the batten in a pleasing curve, bringing it down an equal distance on each side. Mark this curve and cut it out on the band saw. Clamp the pieces in a vise and smooth the curve with a block plane (See photos 1 & 2). Repeat this step for the two end pieces and the handle.

6 Referring to Fig. 2, mark the location of the hand hole; drill out the ends with 1-inch Forstner or spade bit (See photos 4 & 5). *Note: To prevent tearout, drill just until the point comes through the opposite side, then turn the piece over and drill back through the hole from that side.* Join the two holes with a curved line that parallels the top shape; cut out with a jigsaw. Finish inside edges with sandpaper.

PROJECT SIZE
21⅝x9½x6¾ inches

TOOLS
- Table saw with miter gauge
- Bevel gauge
- Flexible batten
- Band saw
- Block plane
- Drill with selection of small wood bits, countersink bit, and 1-inch Forstner or spade bit
- Jigsaw
- Bar clamps
- Bench vise

SUPPLIES
- ½x8-inch pine*: 8 feet
- ⅝x8½-inch pine*: 18 inches
- Sandpaper, up to 180-grit
- Carpenter's glue
- Masking tape
- Fourteen #6 1¼-inch screws
- Ten 1¼-inch nails
- Tung oil
- Varnish

Measurements given are actual, not nominal. Standard nominal lumber will need to be ripped and/or planed to size.

7 Using the table saw, or a handsaw, chisel and mallet, cut a ½-inch-wide dado ³⁄₁₆ inches deep across the center of the bottom piece (Fig. 3). Dry-fit handle into dado and adjust as needed for a snug fit.

8 Clamp sides and bottom/handle assembly together; hold the end pieces in place (See photo 6). If handle does not touch both ends, trim ⅛ inch from the bottom and fit again. Continue fitting and trimming until handle meets the faces of both ends.

9 Disassemble and progressively sand all pieces to 180 grit.

ASSEMBLE & FINISH

1 Fit the handle and bottom together once more, lining them up carefully. Flip assembly over and clamp the handle in a vise. *Note: Use two scraps of wood to protect handle from vise jaw marks. Drill pilot, clearance and countersink holes (Fig. 4) for five evenly spaced screws; glue and screw handle in place. Wipe off any excess glue. Remove from vise.*

2 Clamp sides and bottom/handle assembly in place with two bar clamps. Drill pilot holes for five evenly spaced nails through each side into bottom. Spread a thin layer of glue on each surface; nail sides in place. *Note: If there is any misalignment between the three uprights, sand the ends until they are flush with each other and the end pieces fit.*

3 Temporarily tape ends in place, taking time to line up the bottom and sides of the end pieces with the carcass of the caddy. Use one of the bar clamps to spring the top edges of the sides together slightly to get a good alignment. Drill pilot, clearance and countersink holes through the end pieces into the top ends of the sides and handle; insert screws. Drill the three-step holes through the end into the bottom panel and screw in place. Attach opposite end in same manner.

4 Sand assembled caddy up to 180 grit. Finish with tung oil and varnish following manufacturer's directions. ✦

Spring the batten in a pleasing curve along the top edges of sides, ends and handle.

Mark the curve and cut it out on the band saw.

Clamp the piece in a vise and smooth the curve with a block plane.

Drill out the ends of the hand hole using a 1-inch Forstner bit.

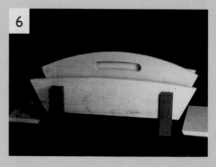
Join the two holes with a curved line that parallels the top shape and cut out with a jigsaw.

Clamp sides and bottom/handle assembly in place with two bar clamps.

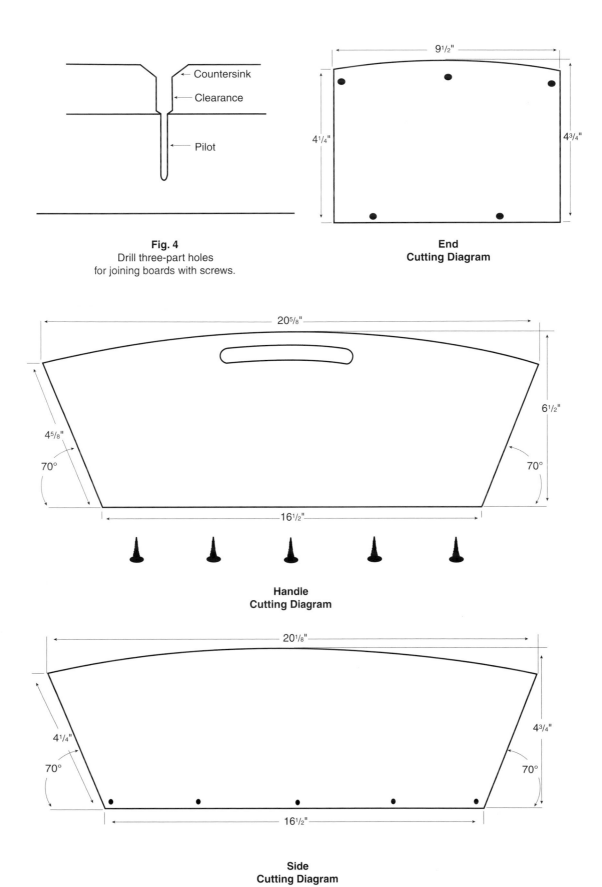

Fig. 4
Drill three-part holes
for joining boards with screws.

← Countersink

← Clearance

← Pilot

End
Cutting Diagram

9½"

4¼"

4¾"

Handle
Cutting Diagram

20⅝"

6½"

4⅝"

70°

70°

16½"

Side
Cutting Diagram

20⅛"

4¼"

4¾"

70°

70°

16½"

OFFICES

If ever a room needed organization, it's the home office. Beautify and simplify with these attractive and functional projects.

DASHING
DESK CLOCK

Design by Loretta Mateik

Rummage through your scrap bin for different species of wood with which to make this unique pen and pencil organizer.

PROJECT NOTES

Walnut dust is toxic. Be sure to wear proper dust protection while cutting this beautiful wood.

CLOCK DISPLAY

1 Set the table saw to rip a width of ¾ inch. Make one cut with the maple to make a piece ¾x¾x13 inches and one cut with the cherry to make a piece ¾x¾x15 inches.

2 Reset the table saw to rip a ⅝-inch width. Make one cut with the walnut to make a ¾x⅝x12-inch piece.

3 Cut all three of the ripped pieces in half lengthwise. Set one half of the walnut aside, leaving a total of five pieces: two ¾x¾x6½-inch pieces of maple, two ¾x¾x7½-inch pieces of cherry and one ¾x⅝x6-inch piece of walnut.

4 Refering to clock display pattern, align these five pieces side-by-side with one end flush; glue and clamp pieces together. Let dry. Sand the face smooth.

5 Transfer clock display pattern to glued-up block. Cut the straight edges with the table saw and the rounded top with the scroll saw or jigsaw.

6 Using the 1⅜-inch Forstner bit, drill a ⅜-inch-deep hole for the clock insert at the location marked on the pattern (centered side to side and 3 inches from the bottom).

7 Rout the front edge of the clock display using the ⅛-inch roundover bit. Sand and wipe clean.

PEN & PENCIL HOLDERS

1 Set the table saw to rip a width of 1¼ inches; rip the remaining 1¾-inch-wide piece of walnut to this width.

PROJECT SIZE
8½x5¾x3¾ inches

TOOLS
- Table saw
- Clamps
- Scroll saw or jigsaw
- Drill press or drill with 1⅜-inch Forstner bit, ¹¹⁄₃₂-, ⁵⁄₁₆-, ⁵⁄₃₂-, ³⁄₃₂-inch bits, and #6 countersink bit
- Router with ⅛- and ¼-inch roundover bits

SUPPLIES
- 1x4 maple: 13 inches
- 1x6 Brazilian cherry: 15 inches
- 1x3 walnut: 12 inches
- E-6000 glue
- Sandpaper
- Graphite paper
- Two 1½-inch drywall screws
- DecoArt Americana matte spray sealer
- 1⁷⁄₁₆-inch mini quartz clock insert with gold finish

2 Reset the table saw to rip a width of 1 inch; rip the remaining 2¾-inch-wide piece of maple to this width.

3 With the 5⁄16-inch drill bit, drill three 1-inch-deep holes in the ¾x1¼x12-inch piece of walnut centered widthwise and positioned at ½ inch, 1¼ inch and 2 inches from one end (Fig 1).

4 With the 11⁄32-inch bit, drill two ¾-inch-deep holes in the ¾x1x13-inch piece of maple, centered widthwise and positioned at 7⁄16 inch and 15⁄16 inches from one end. ***Note:*** *If using a hand drill, clamp the excess length of the walnut/maple to your work surface so it is stable as you drill.*

5 Cut the walnut to 2½ inches long, and the maple to 1¾ inches long.

BASE

1 Rip the remaining 4¾-inch-wide piece of Brazilian cherry to 3¾ inches wide; cut to an 8½-inch length for base.

2 Rout the top edges using the ¼-inch roundover bit set deep enough to leave a 1⁄16-inch reveal. Sand all surfaces.

Organizing **TIPS**

Sort the day's mail at the trash can so you can toss junk mail before it can accumulate in a pile.

ASSEMBLE & FINISH

1 Position the clock unit on the base (Fig 2); outline it lightly with a pencil. Remove. With the 3⁄32-inch bit, drill two evenly spaced pilot holes through the base within this rectangle.

2 Lightly clamp the clock unit back onto the base, turn the base over, and drill back through the pilot holes in the base and into the clock unit.

3 Remove the clock unit again, and redrill the holes in the base using the 5⁄32-inch bit and the #6 countersink bit.

4 Spread a dab of glue on the bottom of the clock unit, then attach to base with 1½-inch drywall screws.

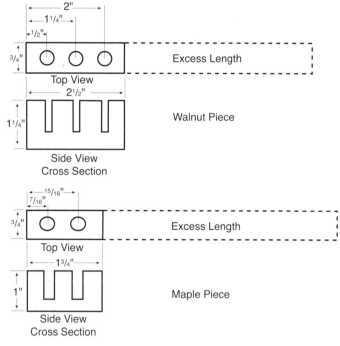

Fig. 1
Placement of Pen/Pencil Holes
Drill holes as indicated,
then cut to length.

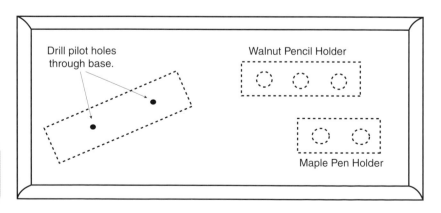

Fig. 2
Placement Diagram

5 Glue the pen and pencil holders in place as shown in Fig. 2, or as desired.

6 Wipe the unit clean of all dust particles and spray with several coats of matte finish following manufacturer's instructions.

7 Add clock insert, pens and pencils. ✦

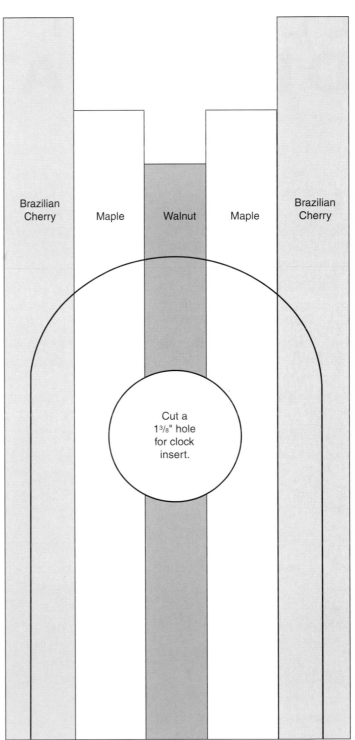

Brazilian Cherry

Maple

Walnut

Maple

Brazilian Cherry

Cut a 1³/₈" hole for clock insert.

Clock Display Pattern

ELEGANT DESK MATE

Design by Joyce Atwood

CUTTING

1 Referring to cutting diagram for ½-inch plywood, cut one 16½ x10-inch piece (for back), one 15½ x2¾-inch piece (for bottom of shelf), one 15½x3¼-inch piece (for bottom), one 15½x5¼-inch piece (for front), one 15⅜x1⅞-inch piece (for drawer front), two 2¾x4¾-inch pieces (for dividers) and two 3¼x7¾-inch pieces (for sides).

Organizing TIPS

Punch a hole in the corner of business cards and thread them onto a shower curtain ring. They can hang on a cup hook near your desk and are easily sorted through.

2 Referring to cutting diagram for ¼-inch plywood, cut one 14⅞x1⅝-inch piece (for drawer back), two 2¾x1⅝-inch pieces (for drawer sides), and one 15⅜x2¾-inch piece (for drawer bottom).

3 Sand all pieces; remove dust.

ASSEMBLE & FINISH

1 Referring to Fig. 1, glue and nail dividers to front. Glue and nail shelf bottom to front and dividers, then glue and nail sides to front. Glue and nail bottom to sides. Glue and nail back to sides, dividers, shelf bottom and bottom.

2 Glue and nail drawer bottom to drawer front. Glue and nail drawer sides to drawer front and bottom. Glue and nail drawer back to drawer sides and drawer bottom.

3 Set nails. Fill holes with wood filler; let dry. Sand pieces smooth; remove dust.

4 Apply one coat of primer and stain blocker following manufacturer's directions; let dry. Base-coat insides and outsides of both assembled units with *black green*; let dry.

5 With damp sea sponge and *glorious gold*, sponge front, back, sides and top edges of organizer; let dry. **Note:** *Do not sponge drawer.*

6 Position rose stencil on front. Stencil petals with *light buttermilk* tipped with *glorious gold*; stencil leaves and stems with *black green* tipped in *light buttermilk*. Let dry. Dry-brush *glorious gold* on tips of leaves. Let dry.

7 Apply satin varnish following manufacturer's directions. Screw knobs onto front of drawer 2¾ inches from each end. ◆

PROJECT SIZE
16½x10x4⅜ inches, including knobs

TOOLS
- Circular saw or table saw
- Nail set

SUPPLIES
- ½x24x24-inch plywood
- ¼x24x24-inch plywood (or scrap)
- Sandpaper
- Wood glue
- ½-inch and 1¼-inch brads
- Wood filler
- DecoArt Americana Satins Primer

and Stain Blocker #DSA34
- DecoArt Americana acrylic paint: black green #DA157 and light buttermilk #DA164
- DecoArt Americana Dazzling Metallics acrylic paint: glorious gold #DA071
- Paintbrushes
- Sea sponge
- Rose stencil
- Stencil brushes
- DecoArt DuraClear satin varnish #DS21
- Two knobs with screws

Add stylish storage to a home office with space for everything: stamps, extra envelopes and, of course, bills!

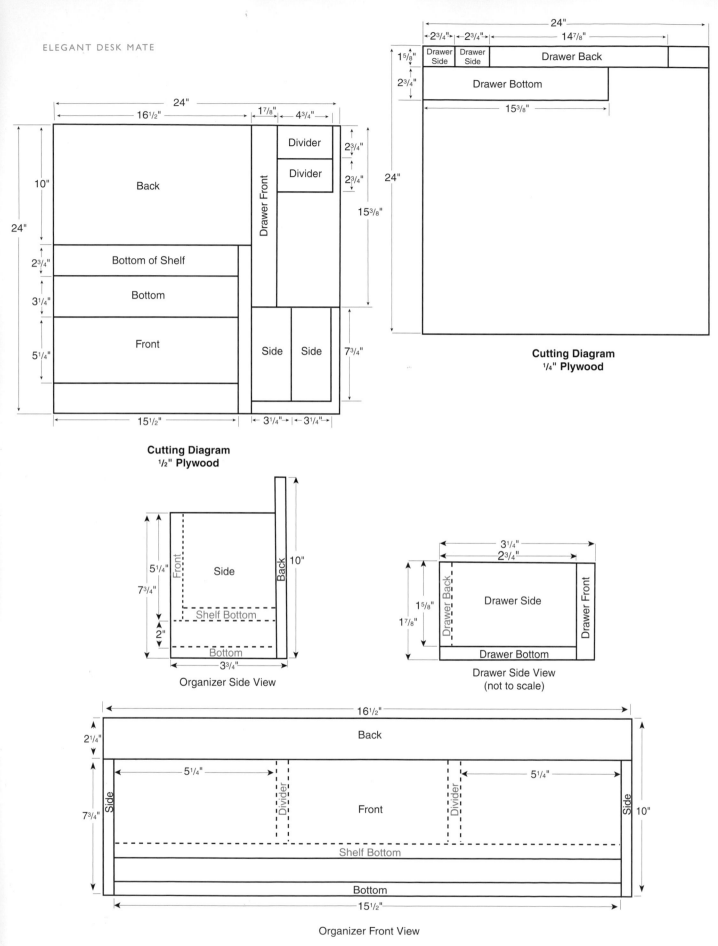

Cutting Diagram
¹/₄" Plywood

Cutting Diagram
¹/₂" Plywood

Organizer Side View

Drawer Side View
(not to scale)

Organizer Front View

Fig. 1

FINGERTIP HELPS

Designs by Anna Thompson

Keep track of pencils, sticky notes and outgoing mail with a desk set made from your scrap wood pile.

Index card/ pencil holder

CUTTING

1 Cut a 15-inch length of 1x8 for this project, then rip to two 3⅛-inch widths.

2 Cut one 3⅛-inch board into two 3⅞-inch lengths for sides and one 5¼-inch length for back.

3 Plane the other board to ⅜-inch thickness and cut it to 5¼ inches for bottom.

4 Rip the remainder to 1¾-inch width, plane to ¼-inch thickness and cut to 6¾-inch length for the front.

5 Mark center of pencil holes on top of sides: Measuring from the back, mark 1⅛, 2⅛ and 3⅛ inches, centered in the width of the side. Drill a 5/16-inch hole 2¾-inch deep at each center. Repeat for other side.

6 Measure up 1¾ inches and mark the front edge of both sides.

From the back, measure in ¾ inch then draw a cut line between the two marks for the side taper. Cut with the band or scroll saw. Sand off saw marks.

7 Measure in 1⅛ inch from each end of the front piece and 1 inch down from the top. Cut a gentle arc between these points. See picture for reference. Sand off saw marks.

ASSEMBLE & FINISH

1 Lap the sides over the ends of the back and glue in place; lap the front over the ends of the sides and glue in place. Glue and set the bottom in place. Clamp and let dry. Be sure to clean off any glue runs now.

Organizing **TIPS**

Store candles in empty cardboard tubes in the freezer. They will last longer and won't break.

PROJECT SIZE

Index card/pencil holder:
 6⅞x3⅛x4⅛ inches
Post-it Notes holder: 3¾x1¾x
 3⅝ inches
Letter holder: 9⅞x2⅛x2⅜ inches

TOOLS
- Table saw
- Planer
- Drill press with 5/16-inch bit

- Scroll saw or band saw
- Clamps

SUPPLIES
- 1x8 wood of choice: one 4-foot length
- Wood glue
- Sandpaper
- Tack cloth
- Spray lacquer

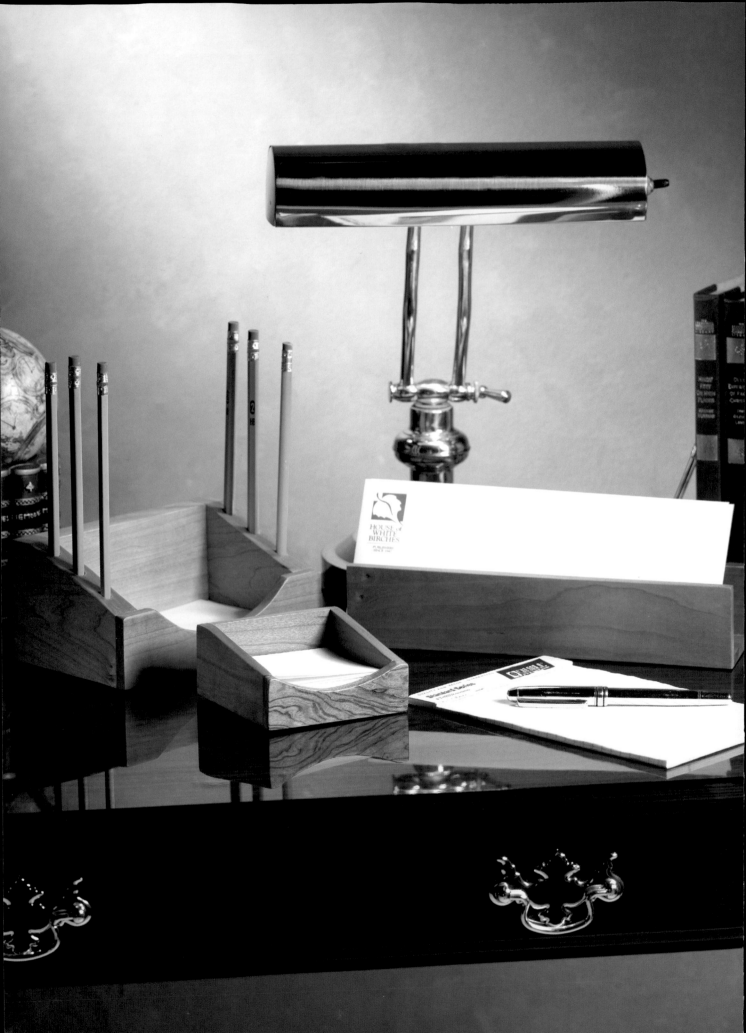

2 Sand all joints flush; remove dust with tack cloth or damp rag. Seal with three coats of spray lacquer, lightly sanding between coats.

Post-it Notes holder
CUTTING

1 Plane the remainder of the 1x8 to ⁵⁄₁₆-inch thickness.

2 Cut a 12-inch length from the ⁵⁄₁₆x7¼ for this project. Rip it to 1¾ inches, then rip again to 3¼ inches.

3 Cut the 1¾-inch width to two 3⅜-inch lengths for sides, and one 3¼-inch length for back.

4 Cut the 3¼-inch width to 3⅛-inches for the bottom.

5 Rip the remainder of the 3¼-inch width to 1¼ inches, then cut to 3⅞ inches for the front.

6 Measure up 1¼ inches and mark the front edge of both sides. From the back, measure in ⅜ inch, then draw a cut line between the two marks for the side taper. Cut with the band or scroll saw. Sand off saw marks.

7 Measure in ⁵⁄₁₆-inch from each end of the front piece and ⅞-inch down from the top. Cut a gentle arc between these points. See photo for reference. Sand off saw marks.

ASSEMBLE & FINISH

1 Lap the sides over the ends of the back and glue in place; lap the front over the ends of the sides and glue in place. Glue and set the bottom in place. Clamp and let dry. Be sure to

clean off any glue runs now.

2 Sand all joints flush; remove dust with tack cloth or damp rag. Seal with three coats of spray lacquer, lightly sanding between coats.

Letter holder
CUTTING

1 Cut a 9⅞-inch length from the ⁵⁄₁₆x7¼ for this project.

2 Rip it twice at 2⅛ inches for sides and once at 1¾ inches for bottom.

ASSEMBLE & FINISH

1 Lap the front and back over the ends of the bottom and glue

in place. Check for square, clamp if necessary and let dry. Be sure to clean off any glue runs now.

2 Sand all joints flush; remove dust with tack cloth or damp rag. Seal with three coats of spray lacquer, lightly sanding between coats. ✦

Organizing **TIPS**

When moving heavy furniture across the floor, flatten some wax milk cartons and put one under each leg. The furniture will slide better and keep the floor from getting scratched.

TOP IT OFF

Design by Anna Thompson

PROJECT NOTES

Sort through the No. 2 white pine 1x8s to find the clearest boards and those with the tightest knots.

MILL WORK

1 Cut 20 inches from one of the 8-foot 1x8s. Plane (or have planed) this 20-inch length and the 6-foot 1x8 to ⅜-inch thickness.

2 Plane (or have planed) to ⅝-inch thickness the 6-foot 1x8, the remaining 8-foot 1x8 and the 76-inch length remaining from step 1.

Organizing **TIPS**

Store garden tools in a small bucket of sand to keep them from rusting.

Note: The ⅝-inch and the ⅜-inch boards have different functions; keep them separate to minimize confusion.

3 With the table saw, rip the 76-inch board and the 6-foot board to 7 inches wide. Rip the 20-inch board to 6½ inches wide.

CUTTING

Note: If you have several boards that require rabbets and a router table is not available to you, it is much easier to rabbet a long piece and then cut to length. If a router table is available, then the smaller lengths are easier to manage and you may wish to cut to length before routing.

1 With the ¼-inch rabbeting bit, rout a ¼-inch-wide by ¼-inch-deep rabbet the entire length of the unripped 1x8.

2 From rabbeted 1x8, use the miter saw to cut two 15¼-inch lengths for sides (B) and two 30-inch lengths for the top and bottom (C).

3 From ⅝x7-inch boards, use the miter saw to cut two 30-inch lengths for the shelves (A).

4 With the ⅝-inch straight bit in the router, set a cut depth of ⁵⁄₁₆ inch. Set the router guide (or table fence) so the full width of the ⅝-inch bit is used. Rabbet both ends of both sides (B) (Fig. 1).

Note: When routing dadoes, always cut the mating pieces at the same time by clamping them together with the ends flush. (See sidebar, page 140.)

5 Remove the router guide. Double check that the router depth is still ⁵⁄₁₆ inch. Referring to Fig. 1, rout the ⅝-inch dadoes for both shelves. Referring to Figs. 2 and 3, rout the ⅝-inch dadoes for the supports on bottoms of the top (C) and top shelf (A), and on tops of the bottom (C) and the bottom shelf (A).

6 Change bits to the ⅜-inch straight bit (keep depth at ⁵⁄₁₆-inch) and rout dadoes in the bottom of the top shelf (A) and the top of the bottom shelf (A) for the dividers (Fig. 3).

PROJECT SIZE
30⅝x15¼x7¼ inches

TOOLS
- Planer (optional)
- Table saw or circular saw
- Router with ⅝- and ⅜-inch straight bits, and ¼-inch rabbeting bit (optional)
- Router table (optional)
- Miter saw
- Compass
- Jigsaw
- Drill with ⅛-inch bit

SUPPLIES
- 1x8 No. 2 white pine: two 8-foot lengths and one 6-foot length
- ¼-inch birch plywood: 2x4 feet
- Pencil and paper
- Sandpaper
- 1¼-inch finish nails
- 1-inch brad nails
- Wood putty
- Wood-Kote Danish walnut stain
- Two 1½-inch wooden knobs
- Deft spray lacquer

Not everyone has room for a rolltop desk, but this sure feels like one! Three drawers and an array of pigeonholes should organize even the busiest household.

CASE ASSEMBLY

1 Dry-fit the shelves (A) into the dadoes on sides (B). Dry-fit the top and bottom (C) into the rabbets. After making any necessary adjustments, measure for the three supports (D, E and F), the three dividers (G) and the back (H). Also measure the height and width of both bottom drawer slots for drawer box.

2 From the ⅝x7-inch stock, cut three supports (D, E & F) to measurements taken. **Note:** *Approximate measurements are 4½ inches for (D), 6⁹⁄₁₆ inches for (E), and 3¹³⁄₁₆-inches for (F).*

3 From the ⅜x6½-inch stock, cut three dividers (G) (approximately 6½ inches long).

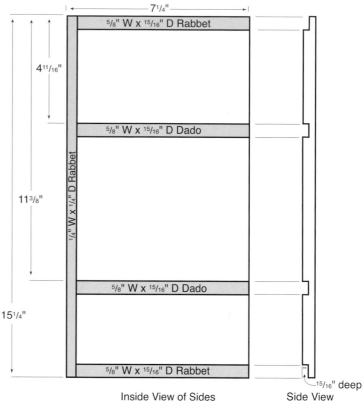

Inside View of Sides   Side View

Fig. 1
Cut ⅝"-wide by ⁵⁄₁₆"-deep dadoes on the insides of the sides and a ¼"-wide by ¼"-deep rabbet at the inside back of each side.

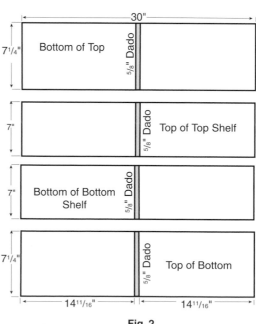

Fig. 2
Rout ⅝" dadoes as shown.

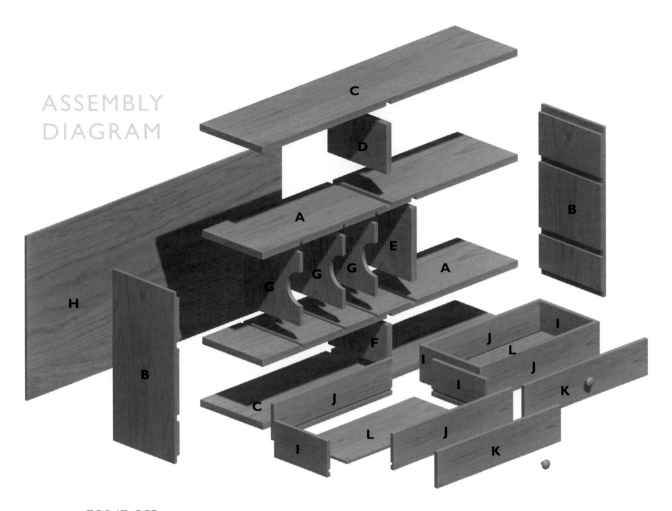

ASSEMBLY
DIAGRAM

TOP IT OFF
(Actual Sizes)

P	T	W	L	#
A	5/8"	7"	30"	2
B	5/8"	7¼"	15¼"	2
C	5/8"	7¼"	30"	2
D	5/8"	7"	4½"	1

E	5/8"	7"	6⁹⁄₁₆"	1
F	5/8"	7"	3¹³⁄₁₆"	1
G	3/8"	6½"	6½"	3
H	¼"	14⅝"	29⅞"	1
I	3/8"	3¼"	6¼"	4

J	3/8"	3¼"	14"	4
K	3/8"	3¼"	14⅜"	2
L	¼"	5⅞"	13⅜"	2

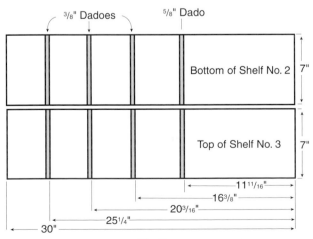

³/₈" Dadoes   **⁵/₈" Dado**

Bottom of Shelf No. 2   7"

Top of Shelf No. 3   7"

11¹¹⁄₁₆"
16³⁄₈"
20³⁄₁₆"
25¼"
30"

Fig. 3
Cut dadoes on the bottom of shelf No. 2
and on the top of shelf No. 3.

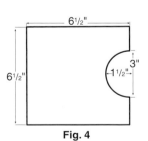

6½"
6½"
3"
1½"

Fig. 4
Cut a 1½"-radius arc on the
front edge of each divider (G).

Dadoes Made Easy

When routing dadoes, always cut the mating pieces at the same time by clamping them together with the ends flush. If they are off even a little it will be noticeable. There are several methods to use. Experiment and find the one you prefer.

Examples of a few of the easier methods are:

1 Make a guide (a jig) that houses both pieces and guides the router.

2 Clamp both pieces together then clamp a straight-edge as the router guide.

3 Use a router table if the deck is big enough and you are careful to keep the pieces against the fence.

Not all router bases are round. Be sure to keep the same place of your router base against whichever guide you use. You can do this by making a pencil mark on the base where it meets the guide when you make the very first cut.

4 From ¼-inch birch plywood, cut piece for back (H) (approximately 14⅝x29⅞ inches).

5 Dry-fit supports and dividers into dadoes on shelves. Make any necessary adjustments. Disassemble case.

DIVIDERS

1 With a compass set for a 1½-inch radius, draw a circle on a piece of paper. Cut this circle out and fold it in half. Place the straight edge along the front edge of one divider and center it vertically. Draw a line around the half-circle and cut it out with a jigsaw (Fig. 4). Sand edge smooth.

2 Using this first divider as a pattern, mark, cut and sand the remaining dividers.

DRAWERS

1 Rip the remainder of the ⅜-inch stock to 3¼ inches. (This will take two passes.)

2 From ⅜x3¼-inch pieces, cut four 6¼-inch lengths for drawer sides (I), four 14-inch lengths for drawer box front/back (J), and two 14⅜-inch lengths for drawer faces (K).

3 Rout a ¼-inch-wide by ³⁄₁₆-inch-deep dado ⅜ inch from the bottoms of drawer sides (I) and drawer box front/back (J). Sand all cut edges to remove saw blade marks.

4 Dry-fit the drawer box together with the front and back (J) butting into the sides (I). Measure the inside width and length, then add ⅜ inch to each measurement. From ¼-inch birch plywood, cut the drawer bottoms (L) just short of those measurements (approximately 5⅞x13⅜ inches).

ASSEMBLE & FINISH

1 Assemble the drawer box with glue and 1¼-inch finish nails.

2 Reassemble the case, including the supports, but not the dividers. Glue all dadoes and rabbets, then finish nail into the shelves from the outside of the sides. Nail the back in place with 1-inch brad nails.

3 Set all nail heads and fill the holes with wood putty. Let dry; sand flush.

4 Following manufacturer's instructions, apply one or two coats of Wood-Kote Danish walnut stain to assembled case, dividers and drawer faces. **Note:** *Do not stain drawer box.*

5 Glue the drawer faces to the drawer box front. In the center (vertically and horizontally) of the drawer face, drill a ⅛ inch pilot hole and attach wood knob with 1¼-inch drywall screw. **Note:** *You will probably find this easiest if you secure the screw with a screwdriver then twist the knob onto it.*

6 Seal with three coats of Deft spray lacquer.

7 Slide dividers into place. ✦

PAPER TRAY
TRIO

Design by Anna Thompson

If you're tired of flimsy plastic in/out boxes, then this is the project for you. As beautiful as it is functional, this desktop unit keeps reams of paper sorted to perfection.

MILLWORK & CUTTING

1 Plane the 1x12 to ⁵⁄₁₆-inch thickness, and the 1x8 to ⁷⁄₁₆-inch thickness.

2 With the radial arm saw, cut the ⁵⁄₁₆x11¼-inch board into three 13-inch lengths for the trays.

PROJECT SIZE
13⅛x9x13⅜ inches

TOOLS
- Planer
- Radial arm saw or circular saw
- Jigsaw
- Table saw
- Miter saw

SUPPLIES
- 1x12 redwood: 4 feet
- 1x8 redwood: 4 feet
- Sandpaper
- Two or six 18-inch clamps
- Wood glue
- ¾-inch brads or copper tacks: 24
- Deft spray lacquer

Organizing **TIPS**

Hang paintbrushes on magnetic knife racks to keep the bristles from getting squashed.

3 Mark the front of each tray at the center, 1½ inches from the front edge and 2⅞ inches from each side. Draw a gentle arc between these three marks (Fig. 1) and cut with the jigsaw. Sand edges smooth.

4 With the table saw, rip the ⁷⁄₁₆-inch-thick board into three 1¼-inch-wide pieces for the tray sides, and one 1½-inch-wide piece for the legs.

5 With the miter saw, cut the 1½-inch piece into four 9-inch legs.

6 Use the miter saw to cut one of the 1¼-inch-wide pieces with mitered corners to frame one of the trays: two pieces each 13⁷⁄₁₆ inches square end to long point, and one piece 12⅛ inches long point to long point. Repeat with the remaining two 1¼-inch-wide pieces to frame the remaining two trays.

7 Sand cut edges of the legs and tray frames to remove unevenness from the saw blade.

ASSEMBLE & FINISH

1 Glue and clamp mitered tray sides to sides and back of each tray, making sure the frame is flush with the bottom of the tray and the front (arc edge) is open (Fig. 1).

2 Measuring from the back to the front, mark 1½ inches and 3 inches on both sides of each tray. Do the same measuring from the front toward the back. Using a square draw a line down the frame sides to use for leg placement.

3 Referring to Fig. 3, use brad nails or copper tacks to glue and nail the legs to the tray sides at the following positions: bottom of lowest tray ¾ inch up; bottom of middle tray 4½ inches up; top of top tray flush with top of leg.

4 Finish with three coats of Deft spray lacquer following manufacturer's instructions. ◆

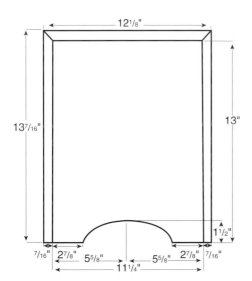

Fig. 1
Cut an arc on the front edge of each tray.
Glue and clamp tray frames to sides
and back of each tray.

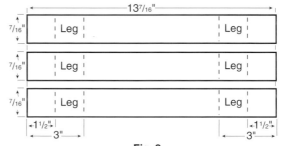

Fig. 2
Mark both sides of each tray
for placement of legs.

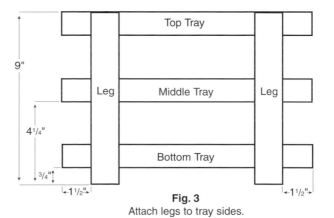

Fig. 3
Attach legs to tray sides.

MIGHTY MINI

Design by Myra Risley Perrin

Bring a casual feel to your home office with this small but useful project.

Note: This project may be built for business cards or notepads, or could easily be altered to allow for other uses: thank-you cards, recipe cards, bills, etc.

PROJECT SIZE
8½x3x5 inches

TOOLS
- Table saw
- Clamps
- V-shaped gouge (other carving tools optional)

SUPPLIES
- ¼x12-inch poplar*: 24 inches
- Wood glue
- Sandpaper: 120- and 220- grit
- Tack cloth
- Acrylic paints
- Clear polyurethane sealer

Measurement given is actual, not nominal. Standard nominal lumber will need to be planed and/or ripped to size. One-quarter-inch birch plywood can be substituted for the poplar.

CUTTING

1 From the ¼x12-inch poplar cut one piece 8½ inches and one piece 15½ inches.

2 Rip the 8½-inch piece into one 4½-inch width for bottom and two 3-inch widths for box sides. Rip the 15½-inch piece into 3-inch widths.

3 Cut the 3-inch-wide pieces to 4½-inch lengths until there are five of them—box front, back and three dividers.

ASSEMBLY

1 Glue the side pieces to the front and back pieces, then glue the bottom piece in place. Clamp together, remove any excess glue and let dry.

2 Space the dividers every 2 inches and glue in place. When dry, remove clamps and sand edges with 120-grit, then 220-grit sandpaper.

3 Use a gouge or other carving tool to add texture or a pattern as

desired. Practice on a scrap piece of wood first to find the detail you are seeking.

FINISH

1 Clean with tack cloth. Paint with acrylic paint (or paints) of choice. Sand edges to give an aged appearance.

2 Seal with clear polyurethane. ✦

BED & BATH

Create a serene oasis in which to escape from the outside world with these projects to enhance the bedroom and bath. You'll find an heirloom jewelry box, a bookcase and hope chest in the ever-popular cottage look, and various organizers for the bath.

Cottage Book Nook
Cottage Hope Chest
Heirloom Jewelry Box
Rolling Storage Cube
Nesting Totes
Shaker Towel Rack
Seashell Corner Cupboard

COTTAGE BOOK NOOK

Design by Cindy Reusser

Celebrate the cottage look in your home and organize books and collectibles with this simple case.

CUTTING

Note: 4/4 lumber (pronounced "four quarter") is a full inch thick. Nominal 1x material is usually only ¾ inch thick.

1 Plane (or have planed) all 4/4-inch red oak to ⅞-inch thickness.

2 Rip one 8-foot board to 2 inches. Mark it No. 1. Rip the other part of it to 2½ inches and mark it No. 2.

3 Rip the other 8-foot board to 3 inches. Mark it No. 3. Rip the other part to 1½ inches and mark it No. 4.

4 Rip the 4-foot board to 1½ inches and mark it for top support. Cut it to a length of 32 inches.

5 Cut No. 1 to two 34½-inch lengths for top front and back frames and two 8½-inch lengths for top side frames.

6 Cut No. 2 into three 30½-inch lengths for front trim pieces.

7 Cut No. 3 to one 36-inch length for base front and two 13-inch lengths for base sides. Cut the remainder of No. 3 to 30½-inches for base front, then rip it down from 3 inches to 2½ inches for bottom filler.

8 Cut No. 4 into two 47¹⁵⁄₁₆-inch lengths for front face frames. Cut back top filler to a length of 32 inches.

9 Transfer scallop pattern 4 times to all three front trim pieces and cut with jigsaw.

PROJECT SIZE
34½x48⅞x12¾ inches

TOOLS
- Planer
- Table saw
- Jigsaw (or scroll or band saw)
- 2-foot (or framing) square
- Clamps
- Router with ¾-inch straight bit
- Router rip guide or straightedge
- Pocket-hole jig
- Drill with ⅛-inch bit and Phillips driver

SUPPLIES
- 4/4x6-inch red oak: two 8-foot lengths
- 4/4x4-inch red oak: one 4-foot length
- ¾-inch oak plywood: one 4x8-foot sheet
- ¼-inch oak plywood or beadboard: one 4x8-foot sheet
- Wood glue
- 1½-inch self-tapping pocket screws
- Finish nails: ⅝-, 1- and 1½-inch
- 1¼-inch drywall screws
- Sandpaper
- Minwax Pastels oil-based pickling stain: winter white
- Clear lacquer or polyurethane

10 Cut and label the ¾-inch oak plywood according to the cutting chart.

DADOES & RABBETS

1 Place two side pieces flat on a flat surface, back edges butted together with tops and bottoms flush. Measuring from the bottom, make a mark on both sides at 2½ inches, 17½ inches and 32½ inches, then draw a line across the width of both boards at each mark. These are the centers of the shelf dadoes. Set the router depth to ⅜ inch, then align the center of the bit with the dado lines. Clamp a straightedge to the sides as a router guide and cut the dado. Repeat this process until all three dadoes are cut in each side.

Note: It is essential that both bookcase sides are cut at the same time to ensure level shelves.

2 Once the dadoes are cut, put the rip guide on the router and set it to cut a ¼-inch-wide by ¼-inch-deep rabbet along the back edge of each

side to receive the ¼-inch case back.

ASSEMBLE

1 Using the pocket hole jig, drive screws through the bottom of the top piece into top side frames, with ends and bottoms of all pieces flush. *Note: Keeping the bottoms flush creates a nice offset (or "reveal") on the top.* Attach front and back frame pieces in the same manner. Set this top assembly aside to use later.

2 Insert the three shelves into dadoes in sides, flush with the front edges of the sides. Glue, if desired, and secure with 1-inch nails from the outside of the sides into the ends of the shelves.

3 Attach front face frames to front edge of sides with tops and outside edges flush. Secure with glue and 1½-inch nails.

4 Align front trim pieces to middle shelves, making sure top edges are flush with the top of the shelf. Secure with glue and 1½-inch nails through front trim piece into the front edge of shelf. Pocket screw each end into the sides of the front face frame pieces. Secure the last front trim piece with pocket screws at the top between the front frames, flush at the top.

5 Align the back top support flush with the top of the sides and the rabbet and attach with pocket screws driven in from the back.

6 Set top assembly in place with back edge flush with the

unrabbeted back edge of the sides and with ½-inch overhang on each side. Secure with pocket screws, two through back of the top support and two through each top side frame, and with screws through the front trim piece into the bottom of the top.

7 Align bottom filler flush with the top of the bottom shelf as with the scallop front on the middle shelves, and attach with glue and 1½-inch nails and with pocket screws into the front face frames.

8 Measure the sides at the bottom. If they measure 11⅞ inches, then miter cut (45 degrees) one base side for each side, 12¾ inches at the long point. For the base front, measure from the long point of one base side to the other base side. Cut the 45-degree miter at both ends to match the side pieces. This should be 35⅛ inches long point to long point. Attach all three of these pieces by predrilling a hole in from the back of the sides and bottom filler, then securing with 1¼-inch screws.

9 Measure for the back, then cut the ¼-inch oak plywood or beadboard to those measurements (approximately 32¾x48 inches).

FINISH

1 Fill all nail holes with wood filler. Let dry. Sand all surfaces and remove dust.

2 Apply stain following manufacturer's instructions. Apply two to three coats of clear lacquer or polyurethane, following manufacturer's directions.

3 Attach back with ⅝-inch finish nails. ✦

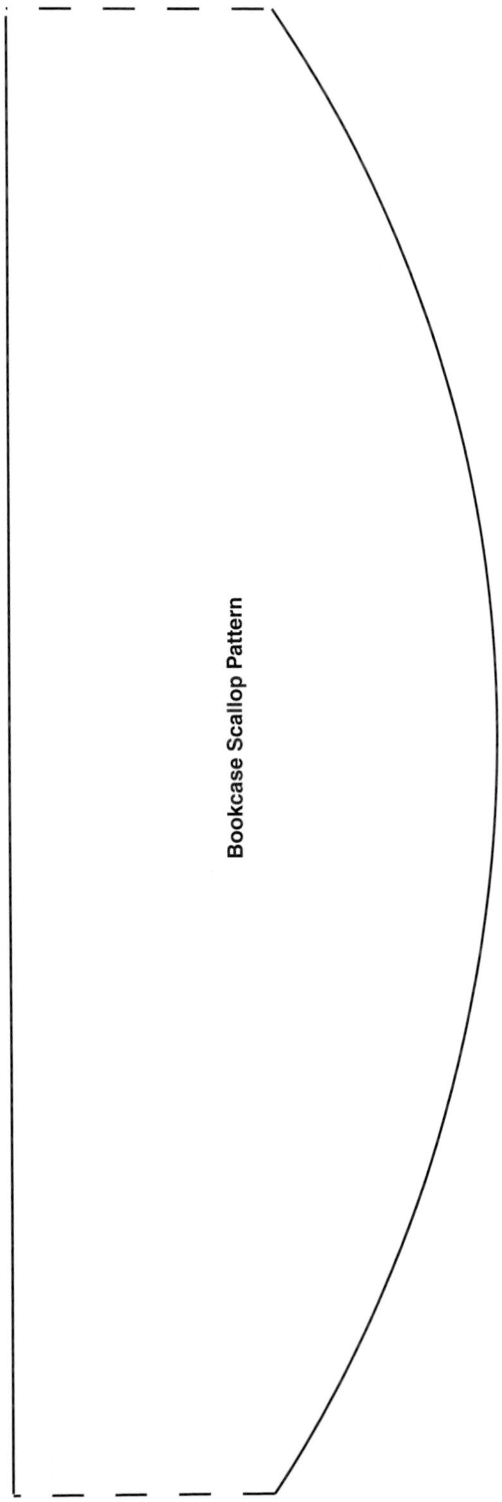

Bookcase Scallop Pattern

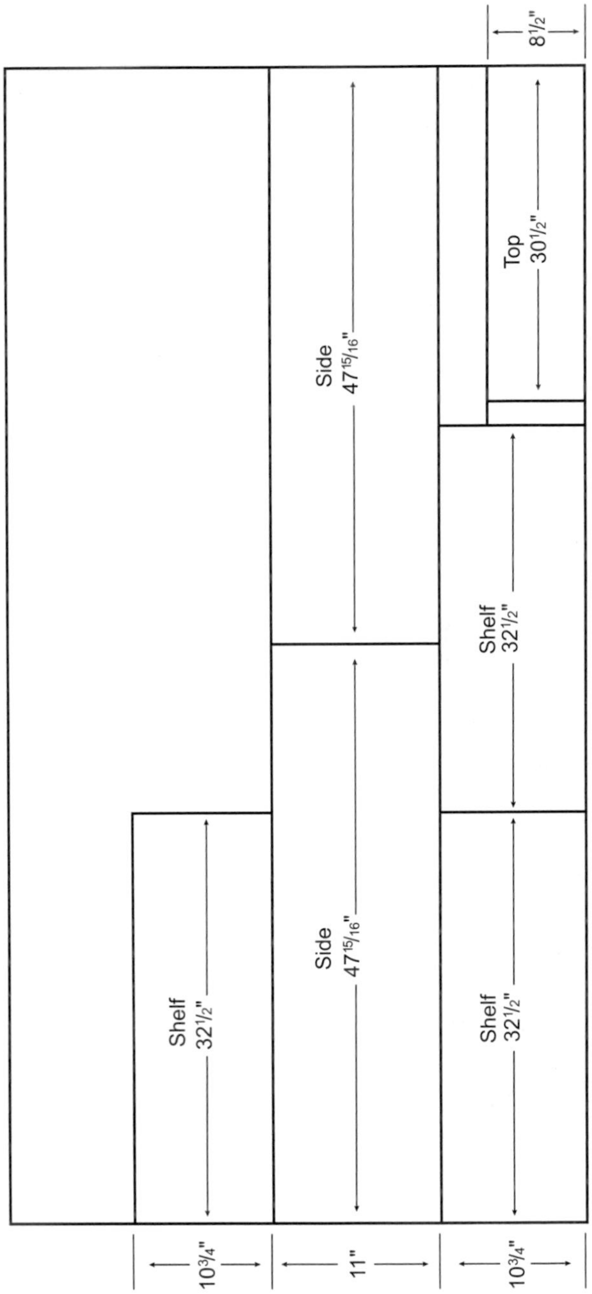

¾" Plywood Cutting Chart

8½"		
Top 30½"		
Side 47¹⁵⁄₁₆"	Shelf 32½"	
Side 47¹⁵⁄₁₆"	Shelf 32½"	
Shelf 32½"		

10¾" 11" 10¾"

Organizing **TIPS**

Attach a towel rack to the footboard of your child's bed. It's a handy place to hang clothes if they are too small to reach the closet rods.

COTTAGE HOPE CHEST

Design by Cindy Reusser

Pickled oak makes a versatile storage chest for quilts, off-season clothes or linens.

CUTTING

Note: 4/4 lumber (pronounced "four quarter") is a full inch thick. Nominal 1x material is usually only ¾ inch thick.

1 Plane (or have planed) all 4/4 boards to ⅞-inch thickness.

2 Rip the 8-foot board to 2 inches. Mark it No. 1. Rip the other part of it to 2½ inches and mark it No. 2.

3 Rip the 6-foot board to 2½ inches, turn it so the factory edge is against the fence, and rip again. Mark one No. 3 and the other No. 4.

4 Cut No. 1 to two 41-inch lengths for lid front frame and lid back frame.

5 Cut No. 2 into two 35-inch lengths for front and back bottom frames.

6 Cut No. 3 to four 17¼-inch lengths for front and back legs.

7 Cut No. 4 into two 18½-inch lengths for side bottom frames. Cut two 16⅝-inch lengths for lid side frames; rip both lid and side frame pieces to 2 inches wide.

8 Transfer the chest scallop pattern to front and back bottom frames and both side bottom frames. Transfer leg pattern to front and back legs. Cut with jigsaw.

9 Rout a ⅛-inch-deep and ¾-inch wide rabbet in the back bottom edge of the lid back frame, beginning and ending 3 inches in from each end to receive the hinge. Chisel corners square.

10 Cut and label the ¾-inch oak plywood according to the cutting chart.

ASSEMBLE & FINISH

1 Using pocket hole jig, drive screws from the bottom of the top piece into top side frames, with ends and bottoms of all edges flush.

Note: Keeping the bottoms flush creates a nice offset (or "reveal") on the top.

2 Attach lid front frame and lid back frame pieces in the same manner.

3 Keeping the insides flush to create an offset on the outside of the chest, attach the legs to the front and back panels with pocket screws from the inside. Attach scalloped bottom frame to the front/back panel assemblies.

4 Attach scalloped side bottom frames to bottom of sides with ends and inside flush. Attach side panels to the front panel assembly from step 3 with the insides flush. Attach assembled back panel assembly to sides.

5 Turn box upside down on a level surface. From scrap 2x4s, cut four 13½-inch pieces. Set these pieces vertically in the corners of the box. *Note: If necessary, use double-sided tape to hold the pieces upright. They will support the chest bottom while you attach it.* Set the bottom into place

Organizing TIPS

Store sheet sets inside their coordinating pillowcases, in the room where they will be used.

PROJECT SIZE
41x18x20½ inches

TOOLS
- Planer
- Table saw
- Jigsaw (or scroll saw or band saw)
- Router with ¾-inch straight or rabbeting bit
- Chisel
- Pocket-hole jig
- Drill with ¹⁄₁₆-inch bit and Phillips driver

SUPPLIES
- 4/4x6 red oak: one 6-foot length and one 8-foot length
- ¾-inch oak plywood: 4x8 feet
- 1½-inch self-tapping pocket screws
- Wood filler
- Sandpaper
- ¾-inch oak veneer iron-on edging tape
- Minwax Pastels oil-based pickling stain: winter white
- Clear lacquer or polyurethane sealer
- 1½x34-inch continuous (piano) hinge
- Two internal side-mount self-balancing spring-loaded lid supports with screws

on the supports. In each corner, measure the distance from the end of the leg to the chest bottom. When the measurements are the same, the chest bottom is level. Attach chest bottom to chest with pocket screws.

6 Set the box upright and band the top edge with the ¾-inch oak veneer iron-on edging tape.

7 Fill all nail holes with wood filler. Let dry. Sand all surfaces and remove dust.

8 Apply stain following manufacturer's instructions. Apply two to three coats of clear

lacquer or polyurethane base on the recommendations of the stain manufacturer.

9 Set lid on top of box with back edge flush with legs. Predrill holes and install piano hinge into the face of the back and the edge of the lid. Make sure screws for back are no longer than ¾ inch.

10 Install lid supports onto each side following manufacturer's instructions for placement. ◆

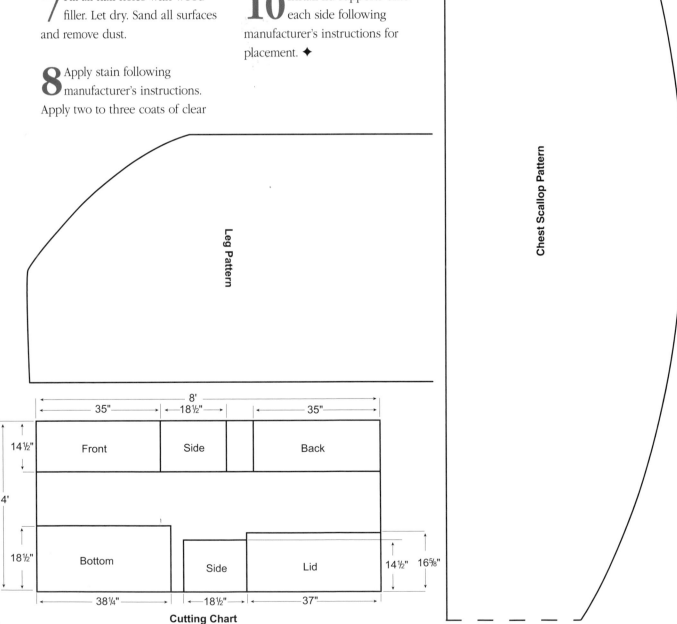

Leg Pattern

Chest Scallop Pattern

Cutting Chart

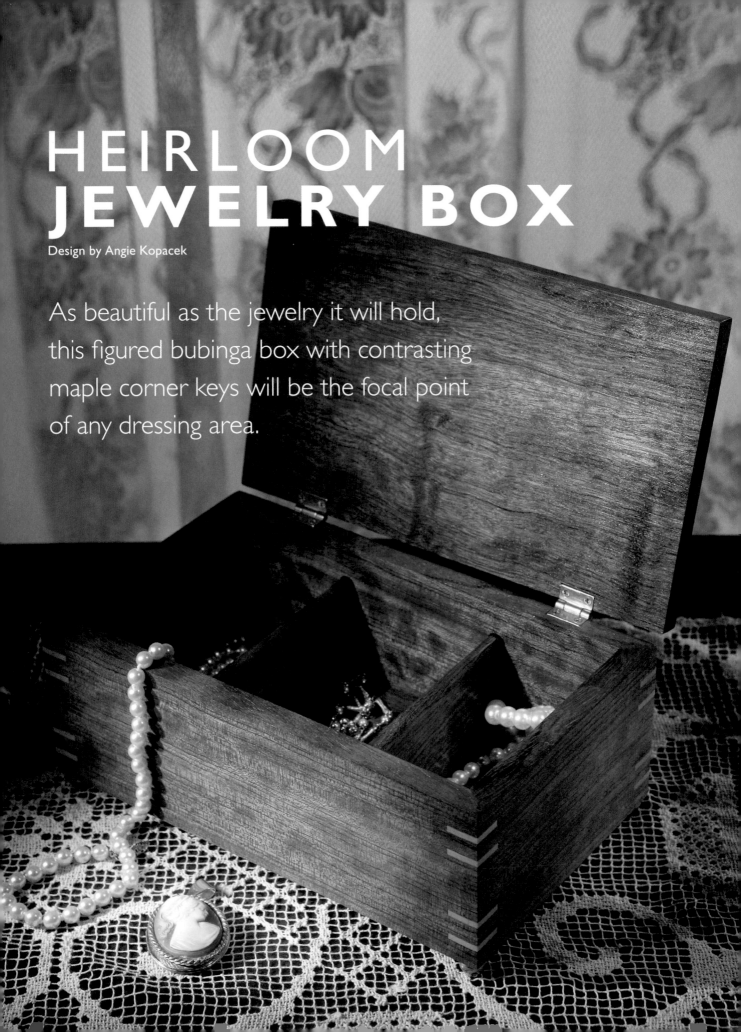

HEIRLOOM
JEWELRY BOX

Design by Angie Kopacek

As beautiful as the jewelry it will hold,
this figured bubinga box with contrasting
maple corner keys will be the focal point
of any dressing area.

PROJECT NOTES

The more teeth a saw blade has, the smoother the cut will be regardless of which saw is being used. It is a good idea to have saw blades sharpened periodically to keep the cut as smooth as possible. Smoother cuts reduce the amount of sanding required.

Whenever you are working with miters, remember that a 45-degree cut will cut away an amount in length equal to the thickness of the board being cut. For this project, the stop is set at 9½ inches from the blade at the fence; the side closest to the fence will measure 9½ inches, but the side away from the fence will measure 9½ inches plus the thickness of the wood being used. It is also easier to measure mitered pieces from the side of the longest angle. This is called a long point measurement. Measuring

from the short point is an option, but it is much easier to get a measurement when you can hook your tape onto an end and extend it.

CUTTING
Front, back & sides

1 From 1x8-inch figured bubinga cut one piece 20 inches, one piece 10½ inches, one piece 9½ inches and one piece 5½ inches.

2 Plane the 20-inch and the 10½-inch pieces to ½ inch thick. Plane the 9½-inch piece to ¼ inch thick. Plane the 5½-inch piece to ⅜ inch thick.

3 On the table saw rip pieces as follows: ½x7¼x20-inch piece into two 3½-inch-wide pieces for front, back and sides; ½x7¼x10½-inch piece to 6½ inches wide for top; ¼x7¼x9½-

inch piece to 5½ inches wide for bottom; and ⅜x7¼x5½-inch piece into two 2¼-inch-wide pieces for dividers.

Front, back & side router cuts

1 Select and mark what you wish to be the outside and bottom edges of ½x3½x20-inch front, back and side pieces. *Note: Usually this would be the edge that has just been cut on the table saw.*

2 Set the fence on the router table so there is ¼ inch between the fence and the ¼-inch straight bit. Set the bit depth to ¼ inch and rout the inside bottom of both the ½x3½x20-inch pieces. This groove will receive the bottom piece.

Front, back & side miter cuts

1 Turn the miter saw to a 45-degree angle. Set a stop 9½ inches from the back edge of the miter saw blade (Fig 1). *Note: Cut a scrap piece of 4-inch-wide wood that is least ¾ inch thick to verify the set-up.*

2 With the outside of the board away from the fence, butt one of the ½x3½x20-inch front/back/side pieces into the stop and make the first cut. Flip the piece just cut end-for-end. With the outside still away from the fence, butt it into the stop and make the second cut (Fig 2). This piece should now be 10 inches long if measured from long point to long point. Mark this piece as No. 1 and set the remainder aside for use in step 4.

3 Repeat step 2 with the remaining ½x3½x20-inch front/back/side

---

PROJECT SIZE
10x4x6¼ inches

TOOLS
- Miter saw
- Planer
- Table saw
- Handheld plunge router with ¼-inch and ⅜-inch straight bits, and 3/16-inch roundover bit (optional ⅛-inch straight bit)
- Band clamp (or two 12-inch clamps)
- Router table (optional)
- ⅛-inch chisel
- Handheld drill with #3 Vix bit and 5/16-inch Forstner bit
- Belt sander
- Random orbit sander
- Drill or drill press

SUPPLIES
- 1x8-inch figured bubinga wood: 5 feet*
- ⅛-inch flat stock maple for contrast
- Sealcoat 2# cut shellac
- Cotton rags
- Yellow wood glue
- Tried and True linseed oil finish
- Woodcraft Brusso hinges #145286
- Woodcraft Brusso feet #145296
- CA glue (cyanoacrylate, or super glue)
- 1200-grit sandpaper

If finding figured bubinga is a challenge, cherry or walnut may be substituted. Be sure to wear dust protection for your lungs.

board. Mark this piece as No. 3 and set the remainder aside for use in step 5.

4 Place the 4-inch-wide scrap piece against the stop. Butt the square end of the 10-inch piece remaining from the board that was cut in step 2 against the scrap piece (Fig. 3). Make the first cut as in Step 2. Flip this piece end-for-end and make the second cut. This piece should measure 6 inches from long point to long point. Mark this piece as No. 2.

5 Repeat step 4 with the piece remaining from the board that was cut in step 3. Mark this piece as No. 4.

Note: Set the 4-inch scrap piece with the 45-degree cut in one end aside for now. It will be used again as support when cutting the corner keys.

Bottom, top & dividers

1 Dry fit the front, back and sides together and clamp in place. Note any changes that need to be made.

2 For bottom, measure the inside dimensions; add ⅜ inch to each measurement, then cut the ¼x5½x9½-inch piece to match these measurements (approximately 5⅜x9⅜ inches). *Note: Adding ⅜ inch to each measurement will make the bottom about ⅛ inch short in width and length. As wood is susceptible to its environment, this shortage will allow for expansion and contraction without becoming too tight or too loose.*

3 Measure the outside dimensions of the clamped box. For top, cut the ½x6½x10½-inch piece slightly

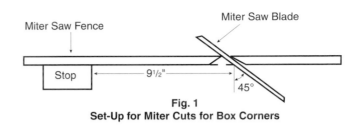

Fig. 1
Set-Up for Miter Cuts for Box Corners

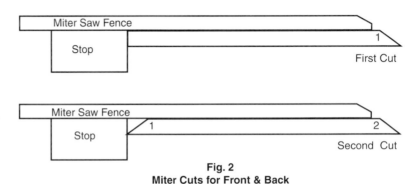

Fig. 2
Miter Cuts for Front & Back

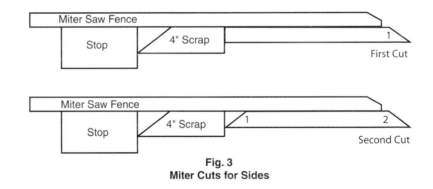

Fig. 3
Miter Cuts for Sides

larger than the outside dimensions of the box. Unclamp the box.

4 Put the ⅜-inch straight bit in the router. Set the router edge guide (or router table fence) to 3 inches. In the front and back pieces only, rout a dado ¼ inch deep by ⅜ inch wide from the dado for the bottom to 2¼ inches from the top. Rout this dado 3 inches in from each end of each piece.

5 Cut the two dividers to the same length as the width of the bottom (approximately 5⅜ inches).

6 With the ³⁄₁₆-inch roundover bit in the router, round over the top edge of each divider. This will allow for a precise fit into the dado.

FINISH & ASSEMBLE BOX BASE

Notes: Finish inside and top of the

front, back and sides, the inside of the lip and bottom, and all of the dividers.

Shellac dries odorless. Oil finishes tend to continue to exude an oil smell for an extended period of time. Shellac also dries quickly and will be sandable within 45 minutes.

1 Dip a soft cotton rag into the shellac and lightly wipe on a thin coat, taking care not to wipe over an area already covered. Apply three coats, letting dry and sanding with 1200-grit sandpaper between coats.

2 Place the box pieces together in numeric order, with piece 2 following piece 1, piece 3 following piece 2, etc.

3 Place the dividers into the dadoes in the front and back.

4 Slide the bottom into the dado near the bottom of each piece.

5 Glue the corners and clamp the box together. ***Note:*** *Be sure there is not glue on or around the bottom or dividers.*

CORNER KEYS

1 Make a corner key jig by taking two similar-sized scrap pieces (1x4s are suggested). Cut a 45-degree angle in the end of one of them; glue the straight end of the other piece to the 45-degree end just cut (Fig 4). This jig allows you to keep the box at a 45-degree angle to the table saw (or router) with safety and accuracy.

2 Set the table-saw fence ½ inch away from the blade, and

the blade ½ inch higher than the thickness of the jig base. Place the box onto the jig and clamp it to the upward angled end. Cut each of the four corners. ***Note:*** *If using the optional router table and ⅛-inch straight bit, set the fence in the same manner, but make four passes for each cut, as taking any more than ⅛ inch at a time with a ⅛-inch bit will break the bit.*

3 Turn the box so you are cutting the opposite end of each corner (if, in the first round you had the top against the table saw fence, then the second round will be with the bottom against the fence) and cut all four corners.

4 Reset the table-saw fence to 1 inch and make the same passes as in steps 2 and 3. You now have four slots in each of the four corners.

5 Cut the maple stock into 16 over-sized triangles (the long side should be around 1¼ inches and the height of the triangle slightly over 3/4 inches).

Glue one triangle into each slot.

HINGE INSTALLATION

1 Along the top back edge of the box, measure and mark 3 inches and 3¾ inches from each side. Next, measure from the back 5⁄16 inch. Mark across both lines at each end of the box (Fig. 5).

2 Using the ⅛-inch sharp hand chisel, mortise the marked area in the top back edge 3⁄16 inch deep.

3 Stack scrap wood spacers at the back of the box to allow the lid to rest evenly with the top of the box back (Fig. 6). Center the lid side-to-side on the box and mark the locations of the hinge mortises on the bottom of the lid.

4 Chisel out the mortises in the lid 5⁄16 inch toward the lid center and 3⁄16 inch deep.

5 Drill pilot holes for the hinge screws with the #3 Vix bit. Install the hinges.

Note: *You may wish to use a gimlet (screw threader) to start threads in the pilot hole. Be careful when installing brass screws; brass is a very soft metal and can snap easily.*

FINISH

1 Use the belt sander to sand the box top and the corner keys flush with the sides and front.

2 With the random orbit sander (or by hand) progressively sand the entire outside of the jewelry box up to 400-grit. The finer the sandpaper grit, the better the oil finish.

3 With a soft cotton rag, wipe a light, thin coat of linseed oil over the entire outside of the box. Wait five minutes, then, with a clean cloth, wipe off the excess oil. Allow to dry for 8 to 10 hours, then buff vigorously with a clean cloth.

4 Repeat step 3 at least twice. The more coats you add, the deeper the shine will be.

5 Turn the box over and rest it on the lid. Measure from each corner in along the miter and make a mark at ⅜ inch. Drill a ¼-inch-deep hole with the ⁵⁄₁₆-inch Forstner bit. *Note: A drill press would be the easiest way to accomplish this, but if one is not available, secure the jewelry box and drill carefully with a handheld drill.*

6 Glue feet in place with CA or super glue. ◆

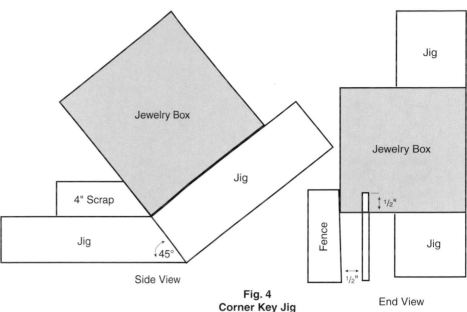

Fig. 4
Corner Key Jig

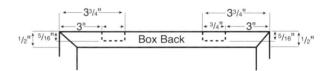

Fig. 5
Mortise Placement for Hinges

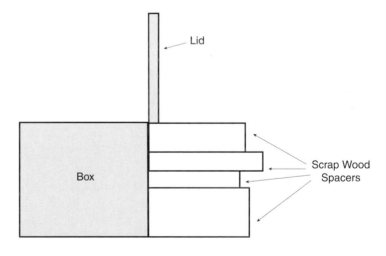

Fig. 6
Set-Up to Mark Lid Placement

Organizing **TIPS**

Keep a set of cleaning supplies in every bathroom of your house. You'll be more apt to "swish and swipe" if you don't have to run around looking for supplies.

ROLLING
STORAGE CUBE

Design by Cindy Reusser

Picking up toys will be more
fun when kids can roll this
cube around the room.

CUTTING

1 From plywood, cut four 18x18-inch pieces for sides, one 18x18-inch piece for top, one 16½x16½-inch piece for bottom and four 2x2-inch pieces for lid stops. Use table saw with miter gauge to cut a 45-degree angle on two opposite edges on each side piece, making sure the angle cuts into the same side of the board.

ASSEMBLE & FINISH

1 Using corner clamps, dry-fit sides so corners meet without gaps. Loosen clamps to remove one side at a time, then glue and nail mitered edges together. ***Note:*** *Mark ⅜ inch from edge and predrill a minimum of three holes per side for nails.*

2 Insert 16½x16½-inch bottom and tap into place so bottom is flush with bottom edges of sides. Glue and predrill; nail into place.

3 Place 18x18-inch top face down on flat surface. Mark ⅞ inch in

from each edge. Glue a 2x2-inch piece at each corner where lines intersect; clamp in place until dry. These pieces keep the lid from sliding off.

4 Set nails. Fill holes with wood filler; let dry. Sand smooth.

5 Prime inside and outside of box and top with latex primer, following manufacturer's directions. Apply one or two coats of latex paint to primed surfaces, letting dry after each coat.

6 Use craft knife to cut star shapes in blank stencil. Position stencil on sides and top of box, stenciling stars in random patterns using desired colors. Let dry.

7 Set cube upside down. Mark placement of casters; predrill holes. Attach casters with ½-inch screws. ◆

Small Star

Medium Star

Large Star

PROJECT SIZE
18x18¾x18 inches, excluding casters

TOOLS
- Table saw with miter gauge
- Drill with 1⁄16-inch bit and Phillips driver
- Four to eight corner clamps
- Nail set

SUPPLIES
- ¾-inch plywood: 4x5 foot piece

- 3D finish nails
- Wood glue
- Wood filler
- Sandpaper
- Latex primer
- Latex paint
- Blank stencil and craft knife
- Acrylic craft paint in three colors (for stars)
- Four 2-inch furniture casters with mounting plates and ½-inch screws

NESTING TOTES

Design by Anna Thompson

Two sets of totes let you start easy with simple butt joints and work your way up to beautiful dovetails!

PROJECT NOTES

This project was built from the bottom up, beginning with the base and building the sides on top of it. While the bottoms of the totes are the same for both sets, the sides will be different. As you work, keep the two sets separate to avoid confusion.

PREP WORK

1 Cut the 6-foot 1x8 into four 18-inch lengths. Glue and clamp long edges of two 18-inch lengths together, alternating end grains, to make two boards each 14½x18 inches. Let dry. These will be used for the bottoms of the largest totes.

2 Plane (or have planed) all boards, including the glued-up boards, to ½-inch thickness.

TOTE BOTTOMS

Note: *Measurements given for thickness and width are actual from this point on.*

1 Cut board lengths as follows:
Small totes—From the 10-foot ½x9¼-inch board, cut two 14½-inch lengths.
Middle totes—From the ½x11¼-inch board, cut two 16-inch lengths.
Large totes—Cut the two ½x14½-inch glued-up boards to 17½-inch lengths.

2 Rip board widths as follows:
Small totes—Rip the two 14½-inch lengths to 9 inches wide.
Middle totes—Rip the two 16-inch lengths to 10½ inches wide.
Large totes—Rip the two 17½-inch lengths to 12 inches wide.

PROJECT SIZE
17¼x9¼x11¾ inches

TOOLS

- Table saw or circular saw
- 18-inch clamps
- Planer (optional)
- Jigsaw
- Router with ⅜-inch roundover bit
- Random orbit sander
- Marking gauge
- Workbench vice and a holdfast
- Dovetail saw
- ½- and ⅛-inch beveled-edge chisels
- Mallet

SUPPLIES

- 1x8 #2 white pine: one 6-foot length and one 8-foot length
- 1x10 #2 white pine: one 6-foot length, one 8-foot length and one 10-foot length
- 1x12 #2 white pine: 4 feet
- Graphite paper
- Wood glue
- 1¼-inch finish nails
- Wood filler
- Sandpaper: up to 150-grit
- Deftoil medium walnut Danish oil finish
- Deft Clear Wood Finish

SIDES
Small tote

1 From the 8-foot ½x7¼-inch board, cut four 14½-inch lengths, two 8-inch lengths, and two 9-inch lengths.

2 Rip all eight of these pieces to 7-inch widths.

Notes: Stack two of the 14½-inch boards and the 8-inch boards with one of the ½x9x14½-inch small tote bottom boards; set aside for butt-joint assembly.

Stack the remaining pieces (9- and 14½-inch) with the remaining small tote bottom board and set aside for dovetail assembly.

Middle tote

1 From the 8-foot ½x9¼-inch board, cut four 16-inch lengths and two 10½-inch lengths.

2 From the 6-foot ½x9¼-inch board, cut two 9½-inch lengths.

3 Rip all eight of these pieces to 8-inch widths.

Notes: Stack two of the 16-inch boards and the 9½-inch boards with one of the ½x10½x16-inch middle tote bottom boards; set aside for butt-joint assembly.

Stack the remaining pieces (10½- and 16-inch) with the remaining middle tote bottom board and set aside for dovetail assembly.

Large tote

1 From the remaining ½x9¼-inch boards, cut four 17½-inch lengths, two 12-inch lengths and two 11-inch lengths.

2 Rip all eight of these pieces to 9-inch widths.

Notes: Stack two of the 17½-inch boards and the 11-inch boards with one of the large tote bottom boards; set aside for butt-joint assembly.

Stack the remaining pieces (12- and 17½-inch) with the remaining large tote bottom board and set aside for dovetail assembly.

Handles

1 Use graphite paper to transfer the handle template to each of the short boards in each stack, centered side-to-side and 1 inch from the top edge. Cut out handles with the jigsaw.

2 Rout both sides of each handle with the ⅜-inch roundover bit.

BUTT-JOINT ASSEMBLY

1 For each tote, butt the short sides into the long ones and secure with glue and 1¼-inch finish nails. *Note: Be sure handles are at the top on both ends.*

2 Turn unit upside down; glue and nail the bottom in place.

3 Set the nails. Fill nail holes with wood filler; let dry

4 Rout all corners and edges with the ⅜-inch roundover bit. Sand joints and sides flush.

DOVETAIL TOTES
Dovetail Layout

1 Begin the layout of the dovetail spacing by drawing the profile of the end of side board for each tote onto paper.

2 Referring to Fig. 1, draw a total of five full and two half dovetails across the ends of the boards for the small and middle totes, and an additional full dovetail for the large tote. Repeat drawings several times until you are satisfied with the pattern. This will be your guide for cutting the dovetails.

Box Layout

1 Layout the box and clearly mark the top edges and the inside. Label each corner piece as shown in Fig. 2.

2 Set marking gauge to the thickness of the wood (½ inch). Scribe all four edges (inside and outside on both ends) of each piece.

Cutting tails

1 For each tote, place the long sides of the tote together with the inside of both pieces facing you. Clamp them vertically in the vise, making sure the ends are flush.

2 With dovetail saw, using the sketch as a reference, start at the point of the angled line and cut down to the scribed line through both pieces at the same time. Continue cutting, working from the end toward the center. Once you have made each cut, turn the boards over and repeat on the opposite end.

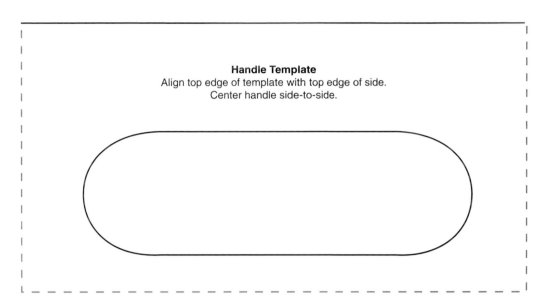

Handle Template
Align top edge of template with top edge of side.
Center handle side-to-side.

3 Remove long pieces from the vise and remove the waste material with a chisel. Do not try to chisel all the way through, but go about halfway from each side. ***Note:*** *Remember, these are the tails, so be sure to keep the part that is widest away from the center of the wood and narrowest toward the center.*

Cutting pins

1 Match up the corresponding corners (a/a, b/b, etc). Butt the short pieces into the long ones, ends flush, and mark the cutouts onto the ends of the short pieces with a very sharp pencil. Mark an X on the part to be removed to avoid confusion.

2 Make these cuts just to the waste side of the lines to assure a snug fit. Gently clean out waste with chisel, taking care not to weaken the pin.

3 Trim the tails of the long sides to fit the socket as necessary. A snug fit, but not too tight, is perfect. ***Note:*** *Do not proceed until you are happy with the fit. If joint is too loose, shim to make it snug.*

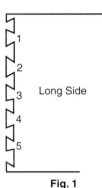

Fig. 1
Draw five full and two half dovetails across ends of long sides for small and middle totes. Draw six full and two half dovetails across ends of long sides for large tote.

Assemble

1 Glue and insert long side pieces into short side pieces. Let dry. Glue and nail bottom in place on each tote.

2 Turn unit upside down; glue and nail the bottom in place.

3 Set the nails. Fill nail holes with wood filler; let dry

4 Rout all corners and edges with the ⅜-inch roundover bit. Sand joints and sides flush.

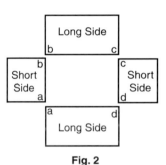

Fig. 2
Layout each tote.
Mark insides and adjacent corners.

FINISH

1 Progressively sand totes to 150-grit; wipe clean.

2 Following manufacturer's instructions, apply one coat of Deftoil medium walnut Danish oil finish; seal with three coats of Deft clear wood finish. ✦

Organizing **TIPS**

Hang a fishnet in your child's room and use tiny colored plastic clothespins to hang artwork or small stuffed animals.

SHAKER
TOWEL RACK

Design by Anna Thompson

Sturdy mortise and tenon joinery make this towel rack beautiful as well as functional.

CUTTING

1 Use miter saw to cut the 1x2 cherry into four 12-inch lengths (B) for bases.

2 From the 1x1¼-inch stock, cut four 35-inch lengths (D) for

PROJECT SIZE
37¼x33¾x12 inches

TOOLS
- Miter saw
- Router with ¾-inch straight bit
- Chisel
- Router table
- Four 6-inch bar clamps
- Four 48-inch bar clamps
- Drill with ½-inch bit

SUPPLIES
- 1x2-inch cherry*: 6 feet
- 1x1¼-inch cherry*: 26 feet
- Wood glue
- Sandpaper

Measurements given are actual, not nominal. Standard nominal lumber will need to be ripped and/or planed to ripped and/or planed to size.

stretchers, four 33-inch lengths (A) for upright pieces and two 7½-inch lengths (C) for cross pieces. Mark the sides of the upright pieces and the cross pieces that will face out.

Tenons

1 Referring to Fig. 1, use router and router table to cut ½x¾x2-inch tenons on the bottom end of each upright piece (A) as follows: Set the depth of the router bit to cut away ¼ inch. Set the router fence 1¼ inches away from the closest edge of the bit and cut all four sides of the upright. Keep moving the fence closer to the bit and make passes over all four sides until all the waste is cleared away.

2 Referring to Fig. 2, cut half-laps on the outside faces of the uprights (A) as follows: Set router bit to cut ½ inch and cut cross-grain from 5 inches to 6¼ inches down from the top on all four uprights.

3 Referring to Fig. 3, with the router bit still set to cut ½ inch, cut half-laps on the inside ends of the two

cross pieces (C). Remove wood from the end to 1¼ inches in from the end.

4 Tenon both ends of each stretcher (D), cutting a ½-inch-long, ¾-inch-wide and ¾-inch-deep tenon, using the same method as when tenoning the uprights in step 1.

Mortises

1 Use router and ¾-inch straight bit to cut ¼-inch-deep dadoes in each 12-inch 1x2 base (B), beginning 2½ inches from each end (Fig. 4).

2 With the mortised sides facing each other, glue and clamp two base pieces (B) together, making sure the glue does not get into the mortise (Fig. 5). Repeat with remaining two pieces. This will result in two pieces, 2x2x12 inches with two mortises clear through them.

3 Remove excess glue and sand thoroughly. Double check to make sure there is no glue in the mortises. On ends of each base, measure 1 inch up from the bottom

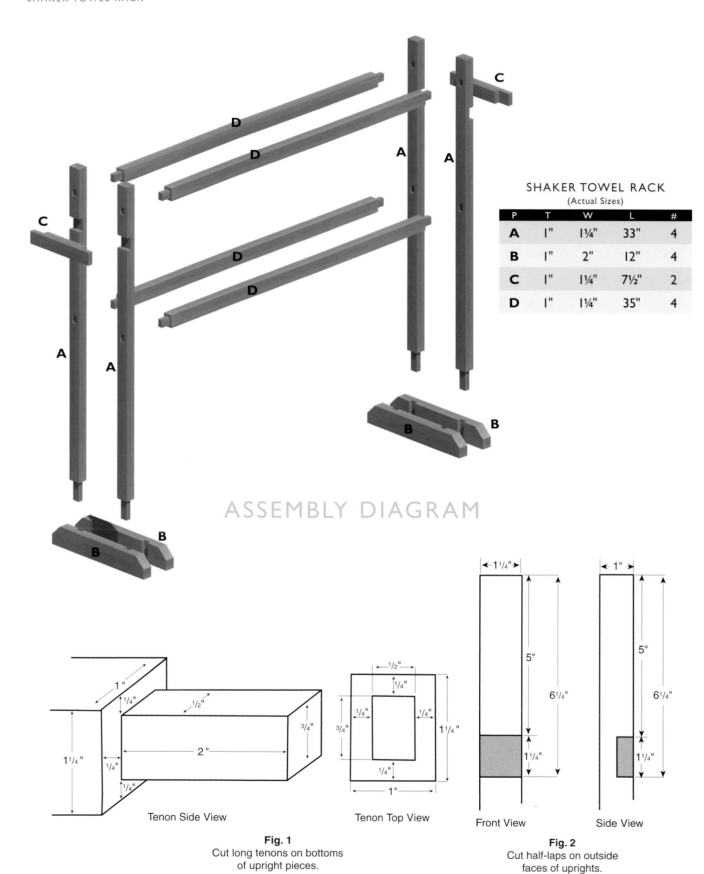

ASSEMBLY DIAGRAM

SHAKER TOWEL RACK
(Actual Sizes)

P	T	W	L	#
A	1"	1¼"	33"	4
B	1"	2"	12"	4
C	1"	1¼"	7½"	2
D	1"	1¼"	35"	4

Tenon Side View

Tenon Top View

Fig. 1
Cut long tenons on bottoms
of upright pieces.

Front View

Side View

Fig. 2
Cut half-laps on outside
faces of uprights.

and cut a 45-degree decorative cut from that mark toward the top (Fig. 6).

4 Lay out the mortises for the stretchers (D) on the inside faces of the uprights (Fig. 7). Cut the mortises ½ inch wide, ¾ inch high, and ¾ inch deep by drilling overlapping ½-inch holes ¾ inches deep, then chiseling out the waste (Fig. 8).

ASSEMBLE & FINISH

1 Trial-fit the assembly and adjust the tenons as needed.

2 Glue the uprights (A) into the mortises on the base pieces (B).

3 Glue and clamp the cross pieces (C) half-lap joints on each upright.

4 Glue and clamp the stretchers (D) in place.

5 Allow to dry, then sand thoroughly.

6 Follow manufacturer's instructions to apply the Danish oil finish. ✦

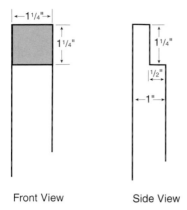

Front View   Side View

Fig. 3
Cut half-laps on inside
ends of cross pieces.

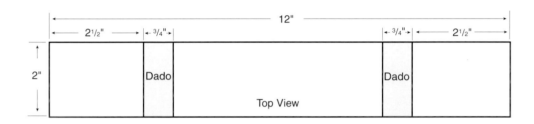

Top View

Fig. 4
Rout ¼" deep
dadoes in ends of
each B piece.

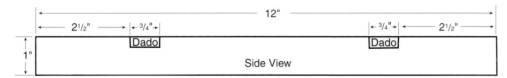

Side View

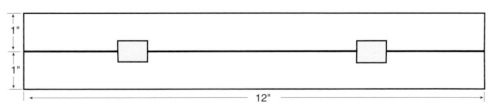

Fig. 5
Glue dadoed pieces together
to make through mortises.

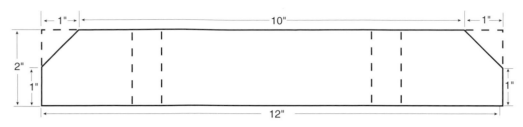

Fig. 6
Side View
Cut 45° angles on
ends of base.

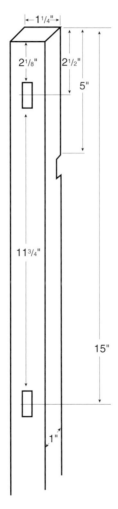

Fig. 7
Cut mortises on the
inside faces of uprights.

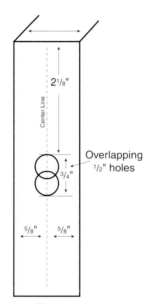

Fig. 8
Cut mortises by drilling two
overlapping 1/2" holes, then
chiseling mortise square.

SEASHELL CORNER CUPBOARD

Design by Delores Ruzicka

Shell cutouts and a soft blue finish bring the feeling of the seashore to your home.

CUTTING

1 Measuring from the back edge, mark the width of one 48-inch board 4 inches at the top and 11 inches at the bottom (Fig. 1). Using the straight edge, draw the cut line between these marks.

2 Measuring from the back edge on the second 48-inch board make a mark 3¼ inch at the top and 10¼ inch at the bottom. Using the straight-edge, draw a cutting line between these marks (Fig. 2).

3 Cut front edges of both boards using a circular saw.

4 Referring to Fig. 3, on the inside of each side, measure down from the top 12¼ inches (A) and 29 inches (B). Using the 2-foot square, draw a line at 12¼ inches and 29 inches from the back edge across the board. These lines will indicate the tops of the two middle shelves.

5 From the 30-inch board, cut one 4-inch length (for top shelf) and one 10¼-inch length (for bottom shelf). On narrow side, measure lengths of shelf lines A and B; cut middle shelves to these lengths from remainder of 30-inch board. *Note: For middle shelves, be sure to measure lines marked on narrow side.*

PROJECT SIZE
11x48¾x11 inches

TOOLS
- 48-inch straight edge
- 2-foot square
- Circular saw
- Scroll saw or jigsaw
- Sander
- Drill with ⅛-inch bit and #6 countersink bit
- Nail set

SUPPLIES
- 1x12 pine: two 48-inch lengths (for sides), and one 30-inch length (for shelves)
- Compass
- Graphite paper
- Twenty-four 1½-inch drywall screws
- Wood glue and brushes
- Four six-penny finish nails
- Wood filler
- DecoArt Americana Satin enamel: evening blue #DSA16 and soft white #DSA02

Organizing **TIPS**

Use a spice rack in the bathroom to contain small cosmetic items.

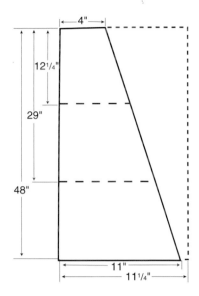

Fig. 1
Cut front edge of wide side.

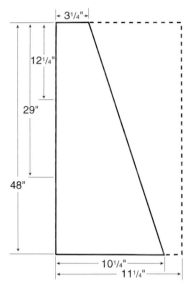

Fig. 2
Cut front edge of narrow side.

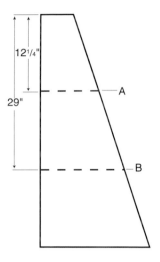

Fig. 3
Mark lines for
two middle shelves
on inside of each side.

6 Use the compass to draw an arc across the front of each shelf. Cut the shelves with a scroll saw or jigsaw.

7 Using the shelf lines you made on the inside of the side board as a reference, lay out the shell patterns and trace using the graphite paper. Cut the shells out with the scroll saw or jigsaw.

8 Sand all cut edges. Hand-sand the shell cutouts. You may need to roll a piece of sandpaper around a dowel or even a pencil to get into the smaller places.

ASSEMBLE & FINISH

1 Butt the narrower side board into the wider one and fasten together using 6 of the 1½-inch drywall screws evenly spaced. Predrill with ⅛-inch bit and #6 countersink bit through the wider side. When you are sure

everything is lined up the way you want it, separate the sides, brush glue on the narrow end and reassemble.

2 Predrill and countersink three holes along the bottom of each side to attach the bottom shelf. Keep the bottom of the shelf flush with the bottom of the sides and the corner of the shelf tight into the corner of the unit. Attach, recheck for satisfaction, detach, glue and reassemble.

3 Fit the top shelf on top of the unit. Check for fit and squareness. If the fit is satisfactory, place a six-penny finish nail in your drill and predrill the top of the shelf. Glue and nail in place with the four six-penny finish nails (including the one in the drill). Use the nail set to sink the nail heads below the surface.

4 Assemble the two remaining shelves by attaching first to one side; using the 2-foot square to make sure the shelf is straight, attach the other side. Be sure the corner is tight into the unit. When all is satisfactory, remove shelves, brush glue on the edges toward the sides and reattach.

5 Fill nail holes in the top of the unit with wood filler; let dry and sand flush.

6 Paint the entire cabinet with *evening blue*. Let dry completely. Use a dry-brush technique to apply *soft white* around each shell cut-out and on the edges of the shelf and cabinet. ◆

Organizing **TIPS**

A wine rack in the bathroom holds rolled towels, stacks of soaps and tubes of assorted stuff.

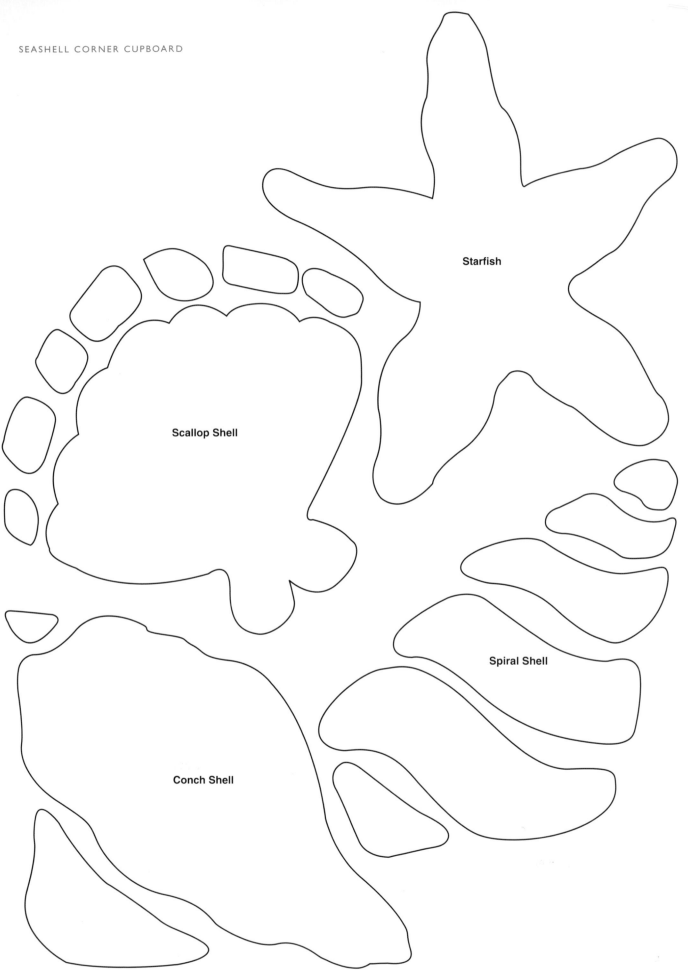

Starfish

Scallop Shell

Spiral Shell

Conch Shell

CONVERSION CHARTS

Standard Lumber Dimensions

NOMINAL	ACTUAL	METRIC
1" x 2"	¾" x 1½"	19 x 38 mm
1" x 3"	¾" x 2½"	19 x 64 mm
1" x 4"	¾" x 3½"	19 x 89 mm
1" x 5"	¾" x 4½"	19 x 114 mm
1" x 6"	¾" x 5½"	19 x 140 mm
1" x 7"	¾" x 6¼"	19 x 159 mm
1" x 8"	¾" x 7¼"	19 x 184 mm
1" x 10"	¾" x 9¼"	19 x 235 mm
1" x 12"	¾" x 11¼"	19 x 286 mm
1¼" x 4"	1" x 3½"	25 x 89 mm
1¼" x 6"	1" x 5½"	25 x 140 mm
1¼" x 8"	1" x 7¼"	25 x 184 mm
1¼" x 10"	1" x 9¼"	25 x 235 mm
1¼" x 12"	1" x 11¼"	25 x 286 mm
1½" x 4"	1¼" x 3½"	32 x 89 mm
1½" x 6"	1¼" x 5½"	32 x 140 mm
1½" x 8"	1¼" x 7¼"	32 x 184 mm
1½" x 10"	1¼" x 9¼"	32 x 235 mm
1½" x 12"	1¼" x 11¼"	32 x 286 mm
2" x 3"	1½" x 2½"	38 x 64 mm
2" x 4"	1½" x 3½"	38 x 89 mm
2" x 6"	1½" x 5½"	38 x 140 mm
2" x 8"	1½" x 7¼"	38 x 184 mm
2" x 10"	1½" x 9¼"	38 x 235 mm
2" x 12"	1½" x 11¼"	38 x 286 mm
3" x 6"	2½" x 5½"	64 x 140 mm
4" x 4"	3½" x 3½"	89 x 89 mm
4" x 6"	3½" x 5½"	89 x 140 mm

Metric Conversions

U.S. MEASUREMENT		MULTIPLIED BY		METRIC MEASUREMENT
Yards	x	.9144	=	Meters (M)
Yards	x	91.44	=	Centimeters (CM)
Inches	x	2.54	=	Centimeters (CM
Inches	x	25.40	=	Millimeters (MM)
Inches	x	.0254	=	Meters (M)
METRIC MEASUREMENT		MULTIPLIED BY		METRIC MEASUREMENT
Centimeters	x	.3937	=	Inches
Meters	x	1.0936	=	Yards

SPECIAL THANKS

We thank the talented woodworking designers whose work is featured in this collection.

Joyce Atwood
Elegant Desk Mate, 130
Handy CD Stacker, 45
Spice It Up, 64

Theresa Ekdom
Snack Time, 60

Barbara Greve
Cheery Apple Towel
    Rack, 80

Sandi Hauanio
Festive Utensil Caddy, 70

Angie Kopacek
Heirloom Jewelry Box, 155
Leisurely Afternoon, 52

Kate Langan
Timeless Tool Caddy, 120

Loretta Mateik
Dashing Desk Clock, 126

Kid's Clutter Keeper, 15
Now You're Cooking, 84
Pogo's Toy Chest, 36
Ready to Go, 13
Ribbon Rainbow, 96

Myra Risley Perrin
Mighty Mini, 145

Cindy Reusser
Among My Souvenirs, 56
Cottage Book Nook, 148
Cottage Hope Chest, 152
Rolling Storage Cube, 160

Delores F. Ruzicka
Seashell Corner
    Cupboard, 171
Wine Glass Holder, 87
Yesterday's Tulips, 26

Bev Shenefield
Crafter's Bonanza, 115
Hang Your Hat, 31

Ready For Action, 99
Stairway Storage, 107

Anna Thompson
Adjustable Book Bench, 48
The Basket Barn, 40
Command Performance, 50
Crafty Roll-Around, 92
Cutlery Keeper, 78
Fingertip Helps, 133
Grandma's Sewing Box, 112
Hanging Catch-All, 20
Nesting Totes, 162
Paper Tray Trio, 141
Shaker Towel Rack, 167
Top It Off, 136
Weathered Window
    Message Center, 75
Welcome Home, 8

Patti J. Ryan
It's A Wrap, 104
Patio Panache, 67